IT'S NEVER TOO early

By Martha Daniel

A families**ALIVE**® Publication

It's Never Too Early
Copyright © 2019 by FamiliesAlive®.
All rights reserved.
Printed in the United States of America.

No portion of this book may be reproduced in any form without permission from the publisher, except as permitted by U.S. copyright law.

For information, address:
FamiliesAlive®
PO Box 3288
Parker, CO 80134
www.familiesalive.org

First edition.

ISBN: 978-1-946853-04-2

10 9 8 7 6 5 4 3 2 1

Dedication

This book is dedicated to my children, Stephen and Keira.

They have been my life-long inspiration and motivation for all I have done in ministry. Their spiritual commitment and growth have always been my #1 goal as a parent. Stephen encouraged me, incessantly, to write this book. My husband, Dave, has faithfully walked alongside me in this parenting adventure.

This book is for them.

Author's Note

My friend, Dan Dupee, says it's not too late to influence your older children because they still need you, even when they think they don't. In his book *It's Not Too Late*, Dan describes the role parents play in shaping the faith of teenagers and young adults.

Because I have spent more than forty years in working with young children and their families, I approach the parents' roles somewhat differently. I say it's never too early to make a positive spiritual impact on our children. In fact, the influence we exert in our children's early years yields a greater life-long response to the Lord by our sons and daughters. This requires intentionality on our part, engaging with the church and other spiritual mentors who can come alongside us in this most-important mission.

Parenting is not for the faint-of-heart. Real challenges and cultural hostilities face our families 24/7. We need focus, guidance, and encouragement to create family environments which foster spiritual growth. The church, partnering with its families, provides the milieu through which spiritual transformation and growth occur.

Foreword

By David Baer, President and CEO, FamiliesAlive®

How can the church most effectively engage moms, dads, and grandparents in the discipleship of their children?

I think this is the most important question that needs addressing today. Something must be done to reverse the disturbing trend of increasing numbers of young adults leaving the church.

Martha has been in the trenches of children's ministry for 40 years making a difference. She knows that children are deeply impacted by their parents – the church can only do so much with the little time they have with a child. So, over the years, Martha has looked for areas in which the church can partner with parents in their spiritual journey with their children. Here are proven ideas for churches of every shape and size.

What you won't find here is any kind of one-size-fits-alll solution. You will not read about the one program or one approach that will be the perfect fit for any family and any church. But what you will find here is a sound Biblical understanding of the role of parents and creative ideas on how children's ministry can also mesh with a proactive family ministry approach in the local church.

FamiliesAlive® has taught for 20 years that moms and dads are the missing link in the process of passing faith to their children. As these things are talked about and emphasized in our churches – just maybe we will see an extraordinary move of the Lord God to revitalize and renew our moms, dads, and grandparents to more effectively minister to their own children. We can all pray that it will be so!

I am delighted to enthusiastically recommend Martha's book.

Contents

1

The Challenge

Why write this book? Why should you invest your time in reading this book?

Over the years I have attended many Children's Ministries conferences with publishers and vendors selling curriculum and ministry tools to make ministry easier, slicker, more entertaining, and even more relevant. Thousands of well-meaning, dedicated volunteers and paid church staff flock to these conferences, seeking new inspiration to sustain them emotionally, spiritually, and vocationally. They're seeking the next big idea that will transform their ministry that, in some cases, has grown somewhat stagnant.

These conferences provide "a shot in the arm" for their attendees, but the glow doesn't last. Attendees go home with a new curriculum in hand, a few new resource books, and the same paradigm for ministry they held when they walked through the doors on the first day. They may have boarded a sailing ship of ministry models designed for ministry success, but perhaps they got on the wrong boat.

Probably the most helpful conference I ever attended was by

invitation-only. At the first gathering, the participants created their own agenda together. As we sat in a circle and forged a plan for our time, excitement welled up inside of us. We created an agenda specifically addressing our felt needs: issues we were currently confronting in our ministries. We were also asked to bring a paper copy of our best practices and program ideas to share with the other participants. This conference allowed us to engage others in addressing our concerns and gave us solutions and ideas for how we might address these concerns back at home. While I didn't employ all of those practices and programs, I did borrow many ideas for my own ministry and others served as inspiration for new initiatives.

I realize that many people serving in the family and children's ministries of our churches don't have access to conferences such as these. Many families do their best in raising their children with the limited resources and support network available to them. My desire in writing this book is to be helpful; to provide practical ideas that can inspire, motivate, and strengthen families and churches. I have no expectation that these ideas will be copied word for word; I hope they will serve as a catalyst for you in ministering to your specific congregation and community. Sometimes, all we need is a good idea.

Today's culture is significantly impacting our churches. Programs that worked for years are becoming less effective than in previous years. New demands require a commitment of time and resources, unlike anything we have experienced in older generations. Respect for Christian truths and values is eroding. How do we equip parents to embrace their faith and help their children sail through the increasingly hostile waters they navigate each day?

We need to be clear about our mission and embrace the Christian values we hold dear. We need to be willing to think about ministry differently than in years past. We need to engage parents in spiritually guiding their children 24/7. And for many people in smaller, less resourced churches, we need ideas that can work for our congregation, no matter its size, status or wealth.

It's Not Too Late

Childhood is such a brief segment in one's lifetime. But when you are in the thick of it, it doesn't seem that way. Parents think they have all the time in the world to connect with, mold, and shape their children. Then adolescence sets in and parents realize that time is brief before their children leave the nest. They also experience the increasing influence of peers and other outside influences upon their children as their own impact seems to wane. By the time your children have reached their teen years, you might think, "It's too late for me to have an influence on my child. I've missed my window of opportunity." But the good news is this: you are still the greatest influencer of your child, should you act upon that truth rather than abdicate responsibilities because you think you are too late to get into the game.

As important as it is to maintain lines of communication and guide your teen in the life decisions he or she is making, especially in their high school years, it is equally important to be proactive in their early years, making the most of every opportunity. As true as it is not too late to significantly impact your son or daughter, it is never too early to become that primary spiritual influencer of your child. In fact, that is the challenge you chose in becoming a parent.

We become who we are, sometimes, as a result of our positive upbringing; others of us become the people we are today in spite of the negative influences in our formative years. Some of us have great role models as parents. Others need to look to some other healthy families as models in our own family of faith. No matter what course our lives have taken, our desire is to do things right. We want to give our children opportunities, encouragement, and guidance to become all they are destined to be. These noble hopes for our children have led many families into quandaries when making decisions about how to allocate their time and resources for their offspring.

Now, let's examine some of the challenges faced by today's families.

Out-of-Control Competition

Opportunities abound for our children. A plethora of inter-esting activities involving music, sports, scouting, academics, dance and more are available to children beginning in their preschool years. There are so many great choices, perhaps too many great choices, requiring costly commitments of time and money in order to flourish. These demands seem to grow year by year.

Erin and Alex are the parents of two elementary-aged boys. Both parents are athletic, and Alex is a school teacher. They are actively engaged in the struggle to find balance with re-gard to sports and the time commitment involved. They have expressed a concern that parents will go to all lengths, even hiring physical trainers, so that their child excels. Lori and Joe echo this same concern in their particular school district. Erin says that it's hard to involve their children in sports that are not year-round commitments involving several nights per week and weekends. Instead of an emphasis on recreational sports, most teams have become highly competitive.

When my daughter was in fourth grade, she decided to give softball a try. She had experimented with dance, soccer, kara-te, and swimming. On the first day of practice, she discovered that the rest of her team had been playing for five years. They asked her where she had been, believing it would be too late for her to play competently... at nine years old! While she did quite well, she quit after that season was over.

Another mom has a daughter in fourth grade. She swims four nights per week and has swim meets every other weekend on both Saturday and Sunday. She insists this schedule is neces-sary if her daughter is to make the high school swim team. The threat of not making the team keeps families in check. Howev-er, the athletic dreams of children do not become a reality for most. There simply aren't enough spaces on the team for ev-eryone. Many children sustain life-changing injuries that cause them to lose the college scholarship they were pursuing. Other children "burn out" from stress. And only a very small percent-age of boys and girls become Olympians or professional ath-letes. What's more, many parents have bought into the myth that if children aren't investing in sports in high school, they may turn to the wrong crowd.

As long as parents give in to these demands of out-of-control competition, their family life will suffer. Who is willing to stand up and declare that "enough is enough"? Parents Erin and Alex have come to that conclusion. For that reason, they decided to involve their boys at a recreational level so that they can spend time together as a family, participate in Sunday worship, eat together, set up their boys for academic success, and form life-changing and ever-growing relationships with Jesus Christ. This action takes courage to go against the flow culturally and to ease the pressure of competition at earlier ages. This action also impacts the prevalent practice of over-scheduling.

Over-Scheduling

Being a parent is a central part of many adults' identity, and most parents feel as though they are doing a good job. However, due to increased pressures on the family, a significant number of parents feel rushed. Pew Research tabulated the percentage of parents who experience the stress of over-scheduling. "In fact, 31% say they always feel rushed, even to do the things they have to do. An additional 53% say they sometimes feel rushed. Only 15% of parents say they never feel rushed. Mothers are somewhat more likely than fathers to say they always feel rushed (33% vs. 28%), but even among fathers, 81% say they feel rushed at least some of the time. And among mothers, full-time working moms (40%) are significantly more likely than those who work outside the home part-time or not at all (29%) to say they always feel rushed."[1]

The demands of athletics are not the only pressure facing our families. More and more activities for children are available, even during the summer break from school. Parents feel pressured to sign up for everything!

Parents Lisa and Peter sat down to schedule their summer plans for the coming year, wanting to visit their out-of-town family. They quickly realized there was not much summer left once the oldest child attends Art Camp, all three kids go to our church Day Camp, and two attend a one-week overnight camp. Usu-

---

1   Pew Research Center, Parenting in America, December 17, 2015: "Satisfaction, Time, and Support."

ally, they attend a VBS at a neighboring church, take a family vacation to the beach and another to the lake. Meanwhile, the three children continue to bring home flyers with more activities for children, beginning at age two. Lisa also voiced the concern that if a parent waits to involve her child until age six or seven, that child will feel behind in her abilities. There is very little time for children to play outside, imagine and explore; most time is spent in organized activities monitored by adults. Take a walk around your own neighborhood. How many children do you see playing on their wooden climbing structures? How many children play pick-up games in the street these days? Those days are long gone.

How do Lisa and Peter address the over-scheduling issue? They shut off electronics at home so they can spend time together. This helps them to feel more connected with their children and with more control of their lives. They limit their children's activities to one sport, one church activity, and one school activity in order to achieve some balance in life. On paper, all sorts of activities sound great—piano lessons, Odyssey of the Mind, swim team, soccer, baseball, softball, dance, karate, hockey, gymnastics and so forth. They assess the demands for each activity before choosing to get involved. Sometimes, the right choice is to just say "no" to something too demanding.

Some friends of mine were blessed with seven children. Early on, they realized scheduling of activities would be a challenge for them. They signed up their three boys for baseball and their four daughters for another similar activity. They still had a great deal of chauffeuring to do, particularly as the children grew and joined traveling teams, but they were all moving in relatively the same direction. You may need to make a few changes in order for your family to move into greater connectedness with each other and with your Heavenly Father.

The Myth of the Blank Slate

When our newborn was first placed in our arms, we were instantly filled with love and the realization that this little being is our responsibility, 24/7, for the next twenty plus years. We were filled with hopes and aspirations for this child and anticipated all the ways we would mold and guide him into adulthood.

We, as parents, sometimes look upon our children as blank slates upon which we imprint our values, beliefs, and world views. But we also soon discover that this child is, in fact, NOT a blank slate, but a little being fully loaded with his own personality and propensities hard-wired into his core. We discover that it is our job to understand this little being and to adapt our parenting style to most greatly cooperate with that personality, thus encouraging and influencing him in his unique development.

I give thanks for parents such as John and Anne who are committed to instilling Christian beliefs and values in their young children. They are in a stage in which they are seeking discernment for what is best in raising their children, preparing them for the different seasons of life they will experience. Regular worship attendance and participation in a small group provide great support and encouragement for them personally. Praying and reading devotionals with their children on a daily basis as well as enrolling their children in our church's preschool also enhance their faith development. These practices, faithfully maintained, provide stability, a sense of rhythm in the routines of life, and security in a child's faith as he or she sees this faith modeled in the lives of their parents.

Cultural Hostility

While our children may not be blank slates personality-wise, researcher George Barna concludes that this current generation, Gen Z, are blank slates spiritually. Recent research from The Barna Group states, "As the cultural cost of being a Christian increases, people who were once Christian only in name likely have started to identify as 'nones', or those with no religious affiliation".[2] As true as there is an increase in the number of "nones" with regard to religious affiliation, there is also an increase in the number of people overtly hostile to the gospel. A young boy from our church had a dream about passing out Bibles at his school and telling people about Jesus. The next day at school he started talking to another classmate about God. She replied, "you aren't allowed to talk about God at

---

2   James Emery White, *Gen Z* (Barna Group, 2018), p. 26.

school." He didn't know what to do. Upon returning home, he shared this experience with his parents who let him know that it is not illegal to talk about God, pray, or even read the Bible. He understands that he cannot force someone else to want to hear, but he can pray and listen for the Holy Spirit to direct him in what he is to say.

When my children were in elementary school, they celebrated Hanukkah and Kwanzaa through artwork and stories, but there was an astounding silence surrounding the Christmas holiday. Believing that "equal time" was reasonable, I asked the school principal if I might set up a creche scene with pertinent information on the historicity of the birth of Christ. She agreed, and I set up that creche scene with an accompanying anthology of stories in the school atrium, for the purpose of giving a fuller understanding of this particular holiday. I opened to the book of Luke, chapter 2 so that all could read the gospel account. When some middle schoolers walked into the atrium, they remarked, "Isn't that illegal?" The short answer is "no." But too many Christians falsely believe that this is true and are thus silenced. That need not be the case. I set up that creche scene every year my children were in that school.

The LGBTQ movement has also created an environment of hostility towards Christians. Because diversity in all forms is to be embraced, holding an opinion based on one's understanding of Scripture is seen as homophobic. Many young people are convinced that lifestyle choices are relative and that there is no right or wrong with regard to sexual orientation and gender identity. To make a judgment is totally unacceptable.

Another hot topic with which each of us must grapple is the racial divide in our country. Many children of minorities continue to deal with the inequities of life; some white teens experience false guilt or struggle to come to terms with who they are. For as much progress we have made as a nation over the decades, there remains a great divide between the races, and it impacts our families, churches, and social groups.

Materialism

Little people, little problems. Big people, big problems. We have all heard that adage, and we all live in the reality of that statement as our children grow. God eases many of us into parenthood through childbirth. As new as the child is to this big world, so is this overwhelming world of parenting new to us. Just as our newborn meets us for the first time, we also are "new-bies" in this parent/child relationship. We then grow and develop as parents as our child grows mentally, physically, emotionally, socially, and spiritually. And change is ongoing. Just as we master, or at least come to expect, certain behaviors, new behaviors arise and the learning curve spikes to a new level. We are constant learners along with our children.

One key learning revolves around materialism. When my son was a young child, we overwhelmed him with toys on his first Christmas. We discovered that he enjoyed playing with the cardboard boxes much more than the actual toys. We learned we could scale back things dramatically. But as he got older, the desire for more expensive, electronic gifts grew. In fact, by the time he was in high school, the desire for a particular cell phone exceeded our Christmas budget.

One parent, Peter, remarked to me that he has long had a struggle with materialism as it pertains to his children. To ask how much "stuff" is needed is almost a moot point. Most "stuff" isn't needed at all; it is wanted. Most of our "stuff" is also under-appreciated because there's so much of it. We get toys from McDonald's, toy stores, grocery stores, friends, church, for special occasions, and for holidays. Advertisements lure our children into this web of materialism. Everything is made to seem way cooler than it actually is. Besides that, we don't want our children to miss out on what their friends may have.

He and his wife have taken some steps to eliminate "stuff" from their lives. One idea involves giving away an old toy when a new toy is received. Another idea focuses on crafts and games the family can do together, thus building relational connectedness as well. Experiences such as sled riding as a family, skiing, bike riding, and other activities also enhance family relationships. I check them out regularly on Facebook; they practice what they preach!

Playing It Safe

Safety becomes a priority in our increasingly dangerous society. Child predators, child abuse, substance abuse, and bullying concern most parents of school-age children. In our ever-changing society, Hannah Rosin argues that "a preoccupation with safety has stripped childhood of independence, risk-taking, and discovery—without making it safer." Children are "less emotionally expressive, less energetic, less talkative and verbally expressive, less humorous, less imaginative, less unconventional, less lively and passionate, less perceptive, less apt to connect seemingly irrelevant things, less synthesizing, and less likely to see things from a different angle."[3] In our desire to protect our children, we can become over-protective of them. We keep our children safe indoors instead of encouraging them to go out and play, but we don't consider the vast dangers associated with video games, the Internet, and other forms of social media adversely affecting our children. Gen Z, according to Barna, has become a generation of "screenagers."

Referencing the Pew Research data, "Most parents say their children participated in some form of extracurricular activity in the 12 months prior to the survey. Sports or athletic activities are the most popular, but at least half of parents say their children ages 6 to 17 have participated in religious instruction, taken music, dance or art lessons, or done volunteer work. Even more parents report that their school-age children watch TV, movies or videos (90%) or play games (79%) on any electronic device on a typical day, and about half of these parents say their children spend too much time on these activities. About eight-in-ten parents with children younger than 6 also say their children have screen time on a typical day, but fewer say their children spend too much time watching videos or playing games on electronic devices."[4]

---

3   Hanna Rosin, "The Overprotected Kid," The Atlantic Monthly, April 2014 (accessed September 2017 by the Barna Group), pl 34-35.

4   Pew Research Center, Parenting in America, December 17, 2015: "Children's Extracurricular Activities."

Social Media

In the November 2, 2015 issue of *Common Sense Media*, the following information was revealed. "A recent study on children's media use finds that teenagers spend an average of nine hours per day on media use (through TV, Internet, smartphones, and so on) for purposes other than school or homework, and that children ages 8 to 12 spend about six hours per day in these activities."[5] Low-income children generally have less access to this technology but utilize these devices readily as they are made available.

One parent, Dan, described to me the challenge of social media in his own home.

> "We held out longer than most, but we finally allowed our middle school daughter to have a phone in seventh grade. We justified it for safety reasons as she was participating in a sport with after-school practices requiring communication for rides. Although she had a phone she could use to make calls and text, we closely controlled the apps installed and did not allow social media apps such as Facebook, Twitter, or SnapChat. As the seventh-grade school year progressed, we saw examples of where it was clear that our daughter was not included in group activities with several friends who were communicating via social media. This was hard on our daughter and hard on us as parents. At the beginning of eighth grade, we allowed our daughter to install her first social media application, SnapChat. Without a doubt, the app has opened opportunities for our daughter to become much more connected with a broader set of friends. This has generally been a positive experience. However, sometimes she will spend more time on her phone than we find appropriate, or use it at inappropriate times. We have had to strongly enforce usage rules for when the phone must not be used, such as a cut-off time of 9:00 pm.
>
> Other parents seemed to have less concern over the dangers of phones and social media. Many parents provided access to these at an earlier age than we thought was

---

5   Common Sense Media, November 2, 2015: "Tweens, Teens, and Screens: What Our New Research Uncovers."

appropriate. As mentioned, it was not uncommon for our daughter to be left out of activities because she was not connected via social media. There were also instances where we thought parents should have intervened when the exclusion was blatant. We suspect the parents were not fully aware of their child's online activities.

In hindsight, although she may have missed some activities, we feel like holding off until seventh or eighth grade was very beneficial to our daughter. At a younger age, it is too easy for a child to be impacted by their insecurities. It is so important for the child to know their value and worth comes from being a child of God, not from online "likes", "friends", and so on. Our daughter needed for this identity to develop and strengthen, while being protected from the pressures of social media. Our daughter might not admit it, but we think there were times when she preferred her status of not being on social media. It gave her an excuse and protection. She could always say 'my parents don't allow that'. We took an approach where we leveraged a number of parental control tools on both Apple iOS and Android devices. This helped avoid having to manually audit usage."

The Attack on Self-Esteem

Parenting can be equated to the first day of school. You prepare by purchasing the supplies and clothes you need. You hold high hopes for the new year: for the impact of positive friendships for your child, for inspiring teachers, for success in their studies. Parents have nine months to prepare for their newborn. They set up the nursery and outfit themselves with the gear they need to meet every demand of their baby. They are filled with hope for the future, anticipating the friendships their children will enjoy, the adults who will significantly influence them, and the direction they will take for their careers. When the big day finally arrives, parents are thrust into their new roles as providers, nurturers, and comforters of their son or daughter. It can be overwhelming from the start. Gradually parents adjust to their new roles, routines are established, and a new rhythm of life unfolds.

Some new challenges face parents when their child begins

school. Up until that point, the child is essentially under his parent's wing. But then he gets on that big, yellow school bus, and a whole new education ensues. He learns language never spoken in the home. He is exposed to media from which he has been shielded by his parents. Classmates of children as young as first or second grade own iPads and are lured by inappropriate content found on television and video games. Sexuality is introduced at an early age through advertisements, and the threat of pornography is only a click or a tap away. Insecurities arise, particularly when weight, acne, braces, glasses, the lack of athletic prowess, or the lack of items associated with financial wealth come into play. Children oftentimes compare themselves unfavorably and unfairly to others. Even if they don't do it to themselves, there are plenty of others who point out their insufficiencies. Contrasting values, particularly between secular and spiritual parents raise another challenge. When a child visits another school friend, their home rules apply, even though they may be contrary to the rules you are upholding in your own home. It is difficult to let go and to not be overcome with concern for the welfare of your child.

During the elementary years, children are largely protected by their teachers and the structure afforded by the school such as assigned classrooms, code of conduct, and the emphasis on inclusion for all students. Even the lunchroom and recess are highly monitored by adults. But when a child reaches middle school, these safety measures are curtailed and the student enters a whole new world of maneuvering through a social network fraught with peer pressures of all kinds. It causes parents such as Jill to feel concern. She worries about how her daughter will fit in as she moves into middle school. She wants to ensure her daughter continues to surround herself with good, supportive friends; friends who share the same Christian values she cherishes. Because it is normal for there to be push-back on the part of adolescents toward their parents, it's important for parents to become less direct in telling their son or daughter what to do, and to become good listeners, engaging them in discussions about situations that arise, coming to a mutually satisfactory solution whenever possible.

Unengaged Parents

As our children grow, they are exposed to other adults formative in their development. Coaches, teachers, and parents hold much in common. We have coaches for our children's athletic pursuits. We trust teachers to impart academic knowledge in a variety of subjects to our growing children. But when it comes to spiritual development, who are our child's coaches and teachers? That responsibility, as designed by God, has been given to us, the parents. The church, also known as the body of Christ, exists, in part, to encourage and equip you to accomplish the most important job ever: the raising of our sons and daughters.

Unfortunately, not all parents are attuned to spiritual realities. Some parents have abdicated their parental responsibilities partially or entirely. At this point, many grandparents have stepped in to provide for their grandchild. Inconsistencies quickly arise between the parenting styles of the parents and grandparents, such as the need for structure, discipline, organization, self-control, and spiritual guidance. For some parents, a lack of understanding of child development and the social and cultural pressures facing their children causes them to react in certain situations rather than having a basis and a plan for dealing with circumstances as they arise. Grandparents are often the unsung heroes of the family who provide much-needed stability for the child.

Addressing the Challenge

By now, you may be feeling a bit overwhelmed by the challenges facing Christian parents and church leaders in today's society. Certainly, the world we live in today looks very different than the one perhaps you grew up in. But it is important not to be naive if we are to change the trend! In the chapters that follow, we will address what the church can do with children and parents to better address these challenges.

2

The Church as Coach

When a boy or girl signs up for a sport, he or she is assigned a team and given a coach. The coach understands the game far better than the team players and serves to impart that knowledge, assisting children in growing their skills so that they can win competitions and achieve their personal best for the team. But the players must do the work: they must practice drills over and over, participate in all the practices, learn the plays, and follow instruction consistently. Players can't just show up when they want or skip practice altogether. That is not tolerated. Team membership requires a commitment, and the more committed a player is, the better her chances for a positive outcome.

God calls the church and parents to work hand-in-hand as spiritual coaches to our children. We are to be His hands, His feet, and His voice, encouraging, inspiring, and equipping children, helping them to develop a Christian worldview in an increasingly post-Christian society. Ideally, when the family and the church work together cooperatively, the child has the greatest opportunity for faith to flourish.

Faith is first and foremost "taught and caught" in the home. But it is crucial that this real and vibrant faith is also "taught and caught" through other significant relationships in the church. One parent, Dan, commented to me about the importance of the church for their family.

"[The church offers] opportunities for our children to grow in their faith and learn about their identity in Christ. The offerings for elementary and middle school children also have provided a safe environment for our children to develop relationships with other like-minded Christian friends. Finally, our daughter has been exposed to a number of very positive role models who have served as her leaders and youth leaders."

Leading Kids to Christ; a Life-Changing Relationship

George Barna conducted a series of studies regarding the age at which people accept Christ as their Savior. These statistics highlight the importance of reaching people for Christ at an early age. "We discovered that the probability of someone embracing Jesus as his or her Savior was 32 percent for those between the ages of 5 and 12; 4 percent for those in the 13-to 18-age range; and 6 percent for people 10 or older. In other words, if people do not embrace Jesus Christ as their Savior before they reach their teenage years, the chance of their doing so at all is slim."[1]

For this reason, evangelism is an important part of our Children's Ministries and Youth Ministries programs at Memorial Park. While the gospel message is present in everything we do, we intentionally invite children to respond to this message in various settings throughout the year; we don't want to assume that everyone already understands the salvation message. Each summer at our church Day Camp, the gospel is again presented over the course of a week. While we realize many children have made a personal response to Christ already, we are aware that many children know very little about Jesus

---

1   George Barna, *Transforming Children into Spiritual Champions* (Ventura, CA: Regal Books, 2003), p. 34.

Christ. We invite each boy and girl into a life-changing and ever-growing relationship with Jesus Christ. Generally, over eighty children respond to the gospel message each year. For some, this is their initial experience in reaching out to Christ. For many, Day Camp provides an opportunity for a recommitment. But isn't that what most of us need, even as adults? We give as much of ourselves to as much of Jesus as we understand. Hopefully, the depth of our understanding and subsequent devotion grows as it should for any developing child. While we understand that Christ's finished work on the cross is complete, our relationship with Him must continually grow in order to be healthy and fruit-bearing.

Becoming His Masterpiece; an Ever-Growing Relationship

In Ephesians 2:8-10, we read, "For it is by grace you have been saved, through faith—and this not from yourselves, it is the gift of God—not by works, so that no one can boast. For we are God's workmanship, created in Christ Jesus to do good works, which God prepared in advance for us to do."

The work of salvation is a gift we receive from the lavish hand of God. We did nothing to deserve such mercy and love, but we are grateful recipients of it. Even though salvation is totally a gift of grace, the work of spiritual formation requires us to cooperate with the Holy Spirit as full participants in His transformative work.

Verse 10 speaks to us of our identity in Christ; we are His workmanship, His masterpiece. For those who struggle with self-esteem, these words communicate our great worth in the eyes of our Creator. He has endowed us with certain abilities and talents uniquely suited to our specific personalities and life situation. His plan for our lives requires our active participation. It is a purpose only we can fulfill. It is our primary responsibility to discern and to live into that plan as an act of our spiritual worship, as described in Romans 12:1. In light of these great truths, if we say that Jesus is Lord, then why are spiritual priorities relegated to last place in our busy schedules?

As more and more activities clamor for our attention, attendance at Sunday worship has been declining in many communities. When I was a child, perfect attendance pins and bars were awarded annually to children who participated fifty-two weeks in the Sunday School. In the early years of my ministry, we were still awarding pins, but they were based upon a percentage of times the child was present in church. Many arguments grew out of the debate about what the percentage should be. Was seventy-five percent too low? Was ninety percent unreasonable? We soon ended the attendance award program. In later years, we considered regular attenders as those who participated two out of four weeks. While we still have plenty of people who fall into that category, the number of once per month attenders is growing. While church attendance does not guarantee spiritual transformation and is not the only metric we should be looking at, fellowship in the body of Christ is important for spiritual growth and thus, this is definitely not a positive trend.

Certainly, faith development isn't simply about creating and participating in programs to meet spiritual needs. However, participation in the life of the church is critical for corporate worship and spiritual growth within the community of faith. Belonging to a body of fellow believers enhances our own personal faith and enables us to serve our communities and our world with the love of Christ corporately. But faith development doesn't happen for one or two hours per week within the walls of a church building. Faith grows as this muscle is exercised in our everyday lives.

Jonathan Morrow, the Director of Cultural Engagement at Impact 360 Institute, describes a framework for building a strong and lasting faith. He calls it the "Three Rs of Worldview Transformation" which includes, reasons, relationships, and rhythms. He says our children "need reasons for faith", "wise relationships" with trusted adults and peers, and "rhythms to help them practice their faith."[2] These daily rhythms are most optimally experienced within the framework of the family as parents model for their children what it means to rely on biblical truth and then to express their faith by setting God-honoring priorities with their time, resources, and energies.

---

2   Jonathan Morrow, *Gen Z* (Barna Group, 2018), p. 100-101.

One parent, Megan, shared with me how her family exemplifies the practice of the three "Rs". This family of five are truly every-week participants in the life of the church. Both mom and dad have assumed leadership roles and are highly influential among their peers. Their children take part in youth group and small group activities during the week, giving them opportunities to build relationships with wise adults who can exercise a positive influence in their lives. They actively grapple with issues the children confront in their everyday lives such as the struggles and dynamics of difficult friendships, peer pressure surrounding social media, and even life and death issues. They discuss the spiritual implications of these problems and work through them as parents, grounded in faith and seeking Gd's wisdom as they faithfully respond to the issues confronting and confounding their children. They keep it real!

As we become counter-cultural, we take a stand against the wave of influences that would diminish our faith and crush our first love in pursuit of lesser things. This requires courage, commitment, and community.

3
What the Church Can Do: Mission & Vision

So, what can the church do, practically, to better disciple parents and children? Many churches make the common mistake of jumping in mid-stream - they hear of successful programs and curriculum that have been used in other locations and jump right in, assuming they will reap the same results in their church. But before we choose what we will do and what we will use, we need to understand who we are as an individual congregation in relation to our own unique community and its myriad needs. Only then can we orchestrate a symphony of relevant ministry that will strike a responsive chord on our audience.

This section is the result of forty-two years of ministry to children and youth. These convictions stem from practical experiences, situations, and changing cultural dynamics I have encountered in the past four decades. Largely, these next pages are my response to the needs I have identified in the churches I have served. I hope these ideas can be helpful to others in crafting their own ministries. By no means are they meant to be a blueprint for success. What works for one church may not be what is needed for another congregation. But these are tried and true ministry ideas, woven with a coherent philosophy explaining why we do as we do. I hope it helps you.

Focus on Needs

You are undoubtedly reading this book because you want to acquire some tools to make your Children's Ministry the best it can be for your own children or for those families under your care. Sometimes we attend conferences with vendors selling their wares and touting their products as the answer to your ministry needs. But do they take into consideration the needs of your community and congregants? Do you even know the needs of your community and congregants?

Assessing needs is the first step in providing relevant ministries to the particular community you serve. Needs fall into two categories; felt needs and real spiritual needs. Understanding both categories of needs is critical in creating relevant ministry. Jumping in mid-stream with the latest program or curriculum published without considering your audience short-circuits the process of creating thoughtful, meaningful programming, tailored to your specific situation.

Start by asking this: What are the top social and demographic trends impacting the family today? And does your ministry to families reflect and address these trends?

According to the Pew Research Center, two-parent households are on the decline in the United States while divorce, re-marriage, and cohabitation are on the rise. Children with less-educated parents and black children are more likely to be living in single-parent households. Research has also discovered that one in six children is living in a blended family. Another factor significantly influencing the family is the number of mothers entering the workforce. In fact, mom is the primary breadwinner in four out of ten families. "The share of U.S. kids living with only one parent stood at 26% in 2014. And the share in households with two parents who are living together but not married has risen steadily in recent years. These patterns differ sharply across racial and ethnic groups. Large majorities of white (72%) and Asian-American (82%) children are living with two married parents, as are 55% of Hispanic children. By contrast, only 31% of black children are living with two married parents, while more than half (54%) are living in a single-parent household."[1]

How does this compare to the families in your church? Ask yourself: How many two-parent households are in our church? How about single-parent, blended, foster, or adoptive families? How many families have a stay-at-home parent? What is the racial/ethnic makeup of our church? What other factors might come in to play, such as remarriage, step-parenting, marital infidelity, unwed parents, grandparents raising grandchildren, in-laws, caring for aging parents, single adult concerns, infertility, adoption, chronic illnesses, disabilities, daycare, lack of spiritual growth, sexual promiscuity, gender identity, LGBTQ issues, emphasis on sports, gangs, bullying, sexual abuse, crime, and prodigal children?

All of these trends affect the families who enter your church doors each week and should be taken into consideration as you evaluate your own programming. Ask yourself: Are we addressing topics relevant to the families we want to reach? Addressing these real felt needs is a means by which we can speak into real spiritual needs individuals wrestle with. Are we offering programs that are affordable and convenient for busy families? Do we provide childcare so that both parents or a single parent can participate?

Tapping into real spiritual needs requires that you teach for transformation. Addressing the anti-Christian culture of his time, Paul exhorts his readers in Romans 12:2 by saying, "Do not conform any longer to the pattern of this world, but be transformed by the renewing of your mind. Then you will be able to test and approve what God's will is—his good, pleasing and perfect will." This process of increasing conformity to Christ is that of sanctification, the transformation of our inner being.

Paul also reminds us in Ephesians 2:8-10 that we have been saved through our faith. And we have been saved for a purpose. "For we are God's workmanship, created in Christ Jesus to do good works, which God prepared in advance for us to

---

1   Pew Research Center, Parenting in America, December 17, 2015.

do." This work primarily begins with the influence we exert with those closest to us, specifically, with our families.

This inner renewal results in the fulfillment of God's perfect will for our lives. In Colossians 1:9-10, Paul calls us to be filled with the knowledge of God's will, "through all spiritual wisdom and understanding" so that we may live lives worthy of the Lord, pleasing him in every way: "bearing fruit in every good work, growing in the knowledge of God." Once again, our families are the primary beneficiaries of our increasing conformity to Christ as we address practical concerns from a well-informed biblical point of view.

Aim to be Effective

I once heard it said that your vision sets forth who you want to be when you grow up, and your mission describes how you will get there.

As it says in Proverbs 29:18, "Without vision, the people perish." Personal development coach Zig Ziglar puts it this way: "If you aim at nothing, you will hit it every time."

When it comes to parenting, we need to have a vision of what our families can become, with specific steps we can take to help our children travel their own spiritual journeys within the family. Part of a class we teach at my church, *Spiritual Parenting,* includes an activity for writing a Family Mission Statement. Michelle Anthony, the creator of *Spiritual Parenting,* suggests the inclusion of all members in the family in crafting this document. Each person contributes characteristics exemplifying the type of family they hope to become. The Family Mission Statement is then framed and prominently displayed in the home, serving as a daily reminder for everyone of what they have committed themselves.[2]

An example of a Family Mission Statement one family in our church developed states the following: "We, the Weitzel family, choose our faith in Jesus Christ as our top priority in all that

---

2   Michelle Anthony, *Spiritual Parenting* (Colorado Springs, CO: David C. Cook, 2010), Session 4.

we do. We show love and respect by encouraging, forgiving, and helping each other, our family, our friends, and our neighbors, near and far. We pray daily in joyful celebration of and in humble obedience to our Good, Good Father." The statement is neither complex nor overwhelming, but it clearly and simply states priorities that will be challenged, addressed, and upheld as the family does life together.

As important as Family Mission Statements for individual families can be, Vision and Mission Statements for our ministries that are clear and concise are invaluable in establishing and empowering the work we do. Below are the vision and mission statements Family Ministries of Memorial Park Church wrote for ourselves:

Our Vision: *To glorify God as a growing family of Christ followers; embraced, healed and restored by Jesus; empowered by the Holy Spirit; joyfully serving our neighbors near and far.*

This is who we hope to be.

Our Mission: *To come alongside parents as the primary spiritual influencers of their children, inviting them into life-changing and ever-growing relationships with Jesus Christ.*

This is how we will get there.

We recognize that we see children one or two hours each week at best. That leaves one hundred sixty-six hours for family time, school, sleep, and extracurricular activities such as sports, music lessons, scouts, and free time. Given that statistic, it's easy to see that the Christian faith will be "taught" and "caught" through the priorities and example of parents. They set the schedule; they are in control to the extent they choose.

Our mission includes both the element of evangelism, helping each child to cross the threshold of faith, and the element of discipleship, enabling each boy and girl to grow in their knowledge, love, and service to Jesus Christ. We are careful to weave these elements into all our programs so that we can touch the hearts of everyone, no matter where they stand in their own spiritual journey. We want to nudge everyone a little closer to God in all that we do.

Putting Vision & Mission into Practice: Case Study

To ingrain the importance of our mission into everything we do in Family Ministries, I added some adjectives to describe the ministry we do, as well as created an easy-to-remember acrostic for our staff and volunteers.

TRU Acrostic (Based on TRU Curriculum)

T = Transformational. We help children cross the line of faith, grow in their relationships with Jesus Christ, and become Christ-centered adults. We seek to present relevant, applicable, and creative teaching in all venues.

"Let your conversation be always full of grace, seasoned with salt, so that you may know how to answer everyone." Colossians 4:6

R = Relational. Our faith *is* a relationship with Jesus Christ. We rely on others to guide, instruct, and encourage us in our walk with Him. Jim Rayburn, the founder of Young Life, encouraged his staff to "win the right to be heard." AMEN! We win that right through the relationships we build. As someone once said, people don't care so much about what you know until they know how much you care.

"All the believers were together and had everything in common. Selling their possessions and goods, they gave to anyone as he had need. Every day they continued to meet together in the temple courts. They broke bread in their homes and ate together with glad and sincere hearts, praising God and enjoying the favor of all the people. And the Lord added to their number daily those who were being saved." Acts 2:42-47

U = Unstoppable. We want children to grasp the power of God in the lives of biblical characters and to experience His power in their own lives. children are able to share their faith, serve, give, and make a difference in the world. We want to give them those opportunities.

"Whatever you do, work at it with all your heart, as working for the Lord, not for men, since you know that you will receive an inheritance from the Lord as a reward. It is the Lord Christ you are serving." Colossians 3:23-24

Adjectives Describing Our Ministry Mission

Christ-Centered: We want everything we do to point others to Jesus.

"I have been crucified with Christ and I no longer live, but *Christ lives in me.* The life I live in the body, I live by faith in the Son of God, who loved me and gave himself for me." Galatians 2:20

Child-Targeted: We need to tailor programs and engage children at their level.

"To the Jews I became like a Jew, to win the Jews. To those under the law I became like one under the law (though I myself am not under the law), so as to win those under the law. To those not having the law I became like one not having the law (though I am not free from God's law but am under Christ's law), so as to win those not having the law. To the weak I became weak, to win the weak. I have become all things to all men so that by all possible means I might save some." 1 Corinthians 9:20-22

Fun: To quote Jim Rayburn's most famous words, "It's a sin to bore a kid with the gospel." AMEN, AGAIN! To make the gospel anything less than utterly compelling is an affront to God Himself.

"But may the righteous be glad and rejoice before God; may they be happy and joyful. Sing to God, sing praise to his name, extol him who rides on the clouds—his name is the LORD—and rejoice before him." Psalm 68:3-4

Safe: We want to provide both physical and emotional safety to all children in our care. We write and uphold policies that ensure safety, and recruit leaders gifted in working with children. All leaders have completed all clearances required by the state; we optimally staff our leader to child ratios in every group.

"I will lie down and sleep in peace, for you alone, O LORD, make me dwell in safety." Psalm 4:8

Gift-Based: Volunteer leaders possess a wide range of giftedness to our ministry. We never ask someone to lead in a way or with a group that may be uncomfortable for them. If teaching is not their gift, leading a small group may be another way to serve. Novices are placed on teams with experienced leaders; no one is left feeling alone.

"There are different kinds of gifts, but the same Spirit. There are different kinds of service, but the same Lord. There are different kinds of working, but the same God works all of them in all men. Now to each one the manifestation of the Spirit is given for the common good." 1 Corinthians 12:4-7

Family-Focused: Besides providing the singular best hour of each child's week at Tru Kids, we want to do all we can to support and equip parents as the primary spiritual influencers of their children.

"Hear, O Israel: the LORD our God, the LORD is one. Love the LORD your God with all your heart and with all your soul and with all your strength. These commandments that I give you today are to be upon your hearts. Impress them on your children. Talk about them when you sit at home and when you walk along the road, when you lie down and when you get up. Tie them as symbols on your hands and bind them on your foreheads. Write them on the doorframes of your houses and on your gates." Deuteronomy 6:4-9

4

What the Church Can Do: Programming

So, now that your mission and vision is established, let's move onto programming. How do we design programs that are purposeful, aligned with your mission and vision, and effective?

Plan Programs with Purpose

As we discussed in the previous chapter, don't make the mistake of jumping in mid-stream with programming. This mistake usually comes from good intentions - churches want to offer effective programs for families and that becomes their starting point rather than doing the preliminary work of assessing needs and creating meaningful mission and vision statements that tend to these needs.

Sometimes church leaders attend conferences and hear about the latest and greatest curriculum, program, or resource that has worked well for someone else and decide that they, too, should give it a whirl. But not everything that works well in one venue necessarily works well in another. Besides that, it's often not what you use, but who it is who leads that makes the difference between success and failure. My old college professor used to say, "We teach people, not curriculum." Her point emphasizes the importance of relationships, of knowing the people we shepherd and our concern for that which matters most to them. We can use many different materials and they all can be effective. A winning combination includes an inspiring leader presenting biblical material creatively and relevantly.

The five pillars of our church are *Worship, Grow, Belong, Serve* and *Give*. Although ministries tend toward one of these five pillars, an effective ministry contains elements of each of these aspects of church life. Mark 12:30-31says this: "Love the Lord your God with all your heart, and with all your soul, and with all your mind, and with all your strength. The second is this: 'Love your neighbor as yourself.' There is no commandment greater than these." If we are worshipping God through who we are and what we have been given, growing in our commitment to and understanding of Him, deepening relationships with one another in our local body, and extending our hands in service to our neighbors both near and far, we are fulfilling the great commandments of our Lord Jesus Christ.

Programs Memorial Park Church Offers

When I began ministry in the 1970s, life was significantly different than it is today. Not as many women were in the workforce; more families were intact; there was more free time and families were involved in fewer organized sports than there are today.

Millennial families are busier than ever with schedules tied to practices, games, lessons, and homework, all crowded into those few hours between school dismissal and bedtime. Carving out time for one more activity into already crazed lives seems hopeless as long as families allow themselves to be victimized by the unreasonable demands of a coach, league, or activity that requires too much from the participants. Only parents can step up and say enough is enough, as the Weitzels expressed in their Family Mission Statement. Faith is not an extracurricular activity; it is their top priority as a family. It is not ice hockey; it is not basketball, soccer, baseball, or swimming. They are striving for balance in an imbalanced culture of competitive sports, academics and other activities. Various interests and pursuits make life rich and meaningful, but what is the top priority for a Christian? It is to love God with all your heart, soul, mind, and strength. It is impossible to live into that commandment yet give Him last place in our weekly schedules.

Here are the programs we provide during the course of a year. Please remember that we are a large church with a large paid and volunteer staff. I do not share these to overwhelm you or to give you a blueprint of exactly what to do, but as an example of what has worked for us and hopefully inspiration for how to develop your own meaningfully-designed programs. Adapt these to your own church situation, as God calls you!

TRU Kids: This is our Sunday morning ministry we provide for children age 2 through grade 5. We strive to make this hour the singular best hour of a child's week, engaging the children in worship and classes that deepen their understanding of "The Big God Story." Small groups foster community and the application of spiritual truths. Offerings are collected and given to missions. In December of each year, the children vote as to how their offering money will be allocated. We encourage their participation in both domestic and international missions. In this way, the children grasp the direct correlation between their generosity and the number of various ministries they can support. We also sponsor a child through an organization called EduNations. Each month, the children collect money for the monthly support of this child. Again, this project makes giving personal, and each child has some responsibility for supporting this child financially.

MOPs and Women's Bible Study Programming for children: Children enjoy stories, crafts, free play, and organized play while their moms grow in their faith.

Breakout: Two eight-week study series are enjoyed by fourth and fifth graders after school; one series is held in the fall, the other in the winter. Children come for pizza, games, and a study designed to deepen their faith. This is their first experience of "youth group" and they love coming to an activity that is meant for "older children." We discuss topics not addressed in depth on Sunday mornings such as the gospel message, sacraments, the Trinity, personal devotions, the five "pillars" of our church, and qualities that are to describe each of us as Christ-followers.

Christmas Pageant: There is a group of students in our church who love to sing and act. We rehearse a pageant which can be taken "on the road" to nursing homes and performed in our church in December. It's a great way to utilize talents in ways that minister to our elderly neighbors, many of whom are far away from their own grandchildren. We consider this a prime act of service during a very busy season and at a time when people are most open to the gospel.

Student Impact Sundays: Bible studies for students in grades 6-12, divided into Middle School, Confirmation (grade 9), and Senior High.

Student Impact Midweek: Middle School Youth Group plus separate Bible Studies for boys and girls meet on various evenings.

Student Impact Mission Trips: Opportunities are provided for domestic and international trips on an every-other-year basis.

Student Impact Weekend Camps: Students gather with teens from around the region for these popular camps held in November and December each year.

Confirmation: A class which extends throughout most of the school year is offered to students in grade 9. Upon completion of all the requirements, a student is welcome to join the church.

Service Projects

We love to select service projects in which the children can actively participate. Each year we encourage families to participate in Operation Christmas Child. We ask parents to take their children shopping for someone who will have no other gift than that which comes in the Operation Christmas Child shoebox. At a time in which avarice reaches its zenith, we offer an alternative that is personal and, oftentimes, life-changing.

Compassion Day: Each spring, Compassion Day affords another hands-on opportunity for children to connect with those less fortunate. Over the course of a month, they collect cookies, chips, gum, bottled water, and fruits for packed lunches. Then we set up an assembly line for constructing sandwiches on a Saturday morning, pack the lunch bags, and deliver them to a near-by homeless ministry.

Summer Projects: Each summer, we arrange for a domestic and an international mission project. We usually collect food, household supplies, or back-to-school items for a local ministry reaching out to "the least, the last, and the lost." Bringing in actual items rather than money is a much more tangible, meaningful offering than money because children don't generally appreciate the value of some change or dollar bills. They do understand the value of a set of markers, or a package of toilet paper. In 2018, we raised money to purchase refurbished bicycles at $22 each so that children in Sierra Leone can safely ride five miles to school instead of walking that distance. Most children own a bike and can relate to biking rather than walking a long distance. We love the idea of kids helping kids.

Summer Surge

From the time a child turns four years old, he or she can participate in *Summer Surge*, our summer camp held on church property.

Junior Camp: designed for children age 4 through kindergarten.

Day Camp: includes all campers between grades 1-5.

Summer Surge Impact: an Adventure Camp for students in grades 5 and 6 as a transitional experience before they can become counselors.

Work Crew and Junior Camp Counselors: span grades 7-9.

Day Camp Junior Counselors: are hired in grades 10 and 11.

Day Camp Senior Counselors: must be in grade 12 or college.

The beauty of *Summer Surge* is that it allows for a continuous camp experience for a boy or girl for nearly all their growing-up years. Year after year, it is the best week of their summer.

Making the Most of Methods & Materials

Many curriculum houses offer engaging material appropriate for children and teens. The single most important criterion to consider is the theological perspective of the material. Here are some guiding questions to help you evaluate your curriculum:

- Is it biblical and true to the teachings of your church?

- Does it provide for a variety of learning styles?

- Is it adaptable to the size of your group?

- Is it creative; will the activities capture children's imaginations, or will it put them to sleep?

- Does the scope and sequence of the material cover the content of the Bible effectively?

- Does the material provide opportunities to respond to the gospel message?

- Are various teaching methods employed such as lecture, discussion, storytelling, large group/small group activities, suggestions for service opportunities and outreach?

Get Organized

I am a strong believer in team ministry for a number of reasons:

The number one reason involves safety. We want all children who come to our programs to be safe physically and emotionally. Having two, unrelated individuals caring for children who have completed all clearances is the best way to ensure this is so.

- The second reason why team ministry is needed involves the maintenance of proper ratios between the children and the number of leaders required. We aim for a 1:3 ratio or better in the Nursery, a 1:5 ratio in early childhood, and a 1:8 ratio in the elementary grades.

- The third reason relates to training. We match experienced leaders with newcomers so that the new leader can learn procedures and skills from the veteran leader. The children are also more comfortable when they recognize a familiar, friendly face.

- A fourth reason concerns giftedness. Because we recognize that not everyone has a gift for teaching, we don't require anyone to teach unless he or she would like to develop that skill. Others who have volunteered for this ministry do so because they love kids. Those people make excellent small group leaders.

- A final reason for team ministry is the built-in structure in place for times when volunteers are unavailable due to illness, vacation, or other commitments. A team is much more easily able to absorb one person's responsibilities when another person is already scheduled to serve that same group. They are able to work out a schedule among themselves without last-minute call-offs.

In our church, we utilize a Large Group/Small Group model for ministry. In addition to being effective for discipleship, it also makes volunteer recruitment much easier. Volunteers don't feel the pressure to prepare every aspect of the lesson every week. Some volunteers who don't have any extra time to prepare can participate on Sunday simply by downloading the Small Group experience on their smartphones.

Community is the glue of retention for volunteer leaders. We believe strongly in gratitude, and try to convey our gratitude to all volunteers throughout the school year. We make sure they have the materials they need to lead their class. We surprise them with tokens of recognition, Leader Huddles with snacks, a Keurig stocked with coffee, tea, and hot chocolate, and a special Volunteer Appreciation Dinner held at the church in February.

Evaluate Effectiveness

A solid ministry team with effective outreach is not created overnight. What's more, a good leader or a good program is never stagnant. We need to look at everything we do with a critical eye and ask, "How can we raise the bar just a little bit higher next time?" Did you notice that I mentioned raising the bar a little bit higher? I'm talking here about tweaking a good program in order to strengthen it. It is important to ask all parties involved to weigh in. Evaluation forms are helpful in asking for honest feedback.

Sometimes we need to do away with an ineffective program or admit that something was an epic fail. A friend of mine coined the term "purge to grow" several years ago. Sometimes we need to stop doing something in order to move in a new direction. Programs that may have been effective a generation ago may have to go. We need to be courageous enough to make that call. Of course, it is much easier to point out programs to drop in the ministry of someone else; it's a little harder to make those same judgments in your own ministry. We can always learn; we can always do better. We never want to plateau. It is then that we start to die.

5

Home Court Advantage: Birth to Elementary School

The Family Ministries mission at Memorial Park Church states that we are to come alongside parents as the primary spiritual influences of their children, inviting them into life-changing and ever-growing relationships with Christ.

As much as we are committed to helping children "cross the line of faith" in Jesus Christ and encouraging them to grow deeper in their love and devotion to Him, we know our influence is small compared to that of the parents. We at church may see children for one or two hours each week at best. Parents do life with their kids during the 168 hours of each week. The sheer amount of time a parent has available to pour into the life of their child is overwhelmingly influential.

Children's Ministry begins with the parents! The patterns they set for their family, the importance they place upon spiritual formation, the balance they achieve in managing crowded schedules and the myriad demands impacting them creates the milieu by which the faith is passed down from one generation to the next.

To live into our mission, we have created a blueprint we call

Home Court Advantage to equip parents so that they can engender faith in their children throughout daily life. We began by creating a list of milestone moments in the life of the family. We then created an opportunity to speak into that milestone experience with the family, heightening their consciousness of the spiritual dimension of this occasion.

The pages that follow outline this blueprint. In the first chapter, we will unpack the Home Court Advantage opportunities available for parents of children from birth through elementary school. In the second chapter, we will cover the opportunities for parents of Middle and High School students.

Spiritual Parenting

Our first offering is a parenting course entitled *Spiritual Parenting*, written by Michelle Anthony, and we encourage all parents to participate in this excellent program. It consists of a series of six DVDs, approximately one hour in length each. Table exercises and group discussion starters are included in each segment.

Spiritual Parenting does not provide steps to create a perfect child. It is not another book with a series of steps to follow or more things to do in order to parent well. Spiritual parenting is about creating environments in your home which will teach the values of responsibility, stepping out of your comfort zone, serving, displaying love and respect, storytelling, knowing the Lord, discovering our identity in Christ, living in the faith community, experiencing course correction, and modeling what it means to be a Christ-follower in daily life.

For example, during the segment on service, Michelle asks the question, *"What needs to be done?"* I print out this simple statement on cardstock for all the participants, encouraging them to place it on their refrigerator at home. They can then teach the concept of serving by talking to their children about opening their eyes to what needs to be done around the house or elsewhere and then becoming a part of the solution to that need. It might mean that the table needs to be set or cleared, the dishes loaded in the dishwasher, or the floor swept. It might also prompt us to return a phone call to someone in need or to come to their assistance in some way. That simple sentence can be used by God to prompt us into action for the good of others and for our own spiritual growth and development.

The C.S. Lewis Institute has published an excellent parenting series entitled *Keeping the Faith; Equipping Families for Effective Discipleship*. This sixteen-week course emphasizes the intentional discipleship of children within the context of everyday life. The practical application of Biblical truths, the development of character, the introduction of spiritual disciplines, and teaching on explaining your faith to others are some of the topics explored in this valuable series.

Welcome to Our World

One of the most anticipated events in the life of a family is the birth of its newest member! The significance and joy of that moment far surpass the preparation for this blessed event. This notable milestone is celebrated with balloons, congratulatory cards, and gifts galore. What a wonderful and key opportunity it is for the church to come alongside the parents in welcoming their child into the world.

We decided that, as the church, we need to be among the first to recognize and celebrate this new life. Wanting to provide an initial means by which we can convey spiritual truths and the love of a Heavenly Father, we purchase CDs of Christian music for children which parents can play in their cars with babies in tow. Not only does the music entertain, but it lays the groundwork of spiritual truth we hope the families will grasp.

We realize that the presentation of the gift is as important as the gift itself. Therefore, our church's Nursery Coordinator arranges for a home-cooked meal to be taken to the family along with the CD. This brief visit allows the Nursery Coordinator and the family to connect with each other and puts a face to the gift. We want the couple to know that they are really important to us and that we want to support them in this new chapter of life. The Nursery Coordinator is now a friendly face to the family and can welcome them at church as she provides comfort and quality child-care for the babies of families in worship.

Baptism

During the first several months of life, many parents choose to have their baby baptized. Recently, we changed the baptism service to be more participatory and celebratory. This new approach has been widely acclaimed.

The parents make initial contact with the Pastor, who then connects with the Nursery Coordinator, regarding their intentions to have their child baptized. The church conducts baptisms three times during the year. Parents select which date works best for their extended family so that all can participate.

Once the new group of children to be baptized is finalized, the Children's Ministries team gets to work. We purchase 8x10 inch picture frames and print the name of each baby in the center of the mat in a colorful, whimsical script. We purchase copies of the book *Zero to One* by Reggie Joiner and Kristen Ivy, which will be used during the baptism class and serve as an insightful resource for parents during their child's first year of life.

One week before the actual baptism, the parents are invited to a one-hour Baptism Class. Upon their arrival, they are greeted by the Nursery Coordinator who provides a brief tour of the Nursery and introduces the parents to those who regularly care for the children on Sunday mornings. The parents leave their babies in the loving care of the Nursery Staff while they attend this brief class.

During the class, the pastor shares about the theological underpinnings of baptism and helps the parents understand the spiritual significance of this action. The Minister to Families then engages the parents with a brief, practical teaching on faith development based on the teachings in *Zero to One*. Finally, we rehearse the ceremony with the parents in the sanctuary so they know exactly where to sit, when to stand, what to do with siblings, and every other question surrounding the ceremony. Before they leave they imprint a personalized picture frame mat with their inked fingerprints, signifying the spiritual impression they desire to make in their child's life. The other parents in the class also imprint their commitment to upholding these parents in their faith promise to raise their child to know, love, and serve the Lord Jesus Christ. Each couple is asked to write a letter to their son or daughter, speaking about the hopes and dreams they possess for their child. This letter is to be placed behind the photograph of the matted frame for safe-keeping.

On baptism morning, the parents arrive early to take a family photo before entering the sanctuary. The families are invited to the front of the church and each child is individually baptized by the pastor. The culmination of the ceremony occurs as the newly baptized parade down the aisles of the sanctuary. Congregants are invited to imprint the mats of the picture frames following the service as a visible sign that they commit themselves to pray for and make an imprint on this child's life spiritually.

Following the service, a celebratory reception is held for everyone. Throughout the next week, we develop the photographs and assemble the matted frames with the parents' letter to the child placed inside the backing. The photos and the Baptism Certificates are then available for pick-up the next Sunday. We do this so as to encourage parents to come back and make regular attendance in worship part of their family experience.

My First Bible

As much as music plays an integral part in your child's life beginning at birth, so reading God's Word to your children builds God's truth into their lives as they mature developmentally and are able to enjoy stories and books.

Reading storybooks is a favorite activity for parents and children. Parents love reading because it is a great way to calm children, especially at bedtime. Children love reading because they think they are getting to stay up just a little bit longer when they coax their parents to read "just one more book." Reading to your child can begin early in life; certainly, by the time they are two years old, they can engage in this activity. Bible reading is a valuable practice to develop. Including the Bible as the final story of your own storytime ingrains this habit at an early age.

We present a child's first Bible to parents and children on a Sunday morning in the spring of their second year of life. We hold this brief ceremony between our church services so that everyone can attend.

Prayer and Blessings

During Sunday mornings in the spring, we offer *Home Court Advantage* events for parents. The purpose of these gatherings is to equip parents to engage their children in spiritual formation within the rhythm of daily life. These brief sessions introduce parents to resources and methods by which these activities can occur naturally throughout the day. We also teach parents how to bless their children, using the blessings found in our curriculum.

The curriculum we use also has excellent ideas for extending the learning that has taken place at church. We encourage parents to use this resource with their children during the week. It also contains a "blessing for the week." Imagine how powerful those words of blessing can be to your child as she prepares to leave for school each morning, knowing that the Lord is going before her, and her parents are praying for her day. Imagine how faith-producing it is to review your child's day with him, noticing ways in which the Lord has blessed him, guided, or helped him throughout the day. This conscious activity is a great way to strengthen a child's faith, by recognizing God at work throughout the day.

Other helpful tools for prayer include a prayer binder and a prayer journal. A binder can be a series of photographs of specific people for whom you are praying. This group may include family members, neighbors, school teachers, church staff, friends, missionaries, and others currently in need of prayer. Sometimes putting a "face" with a name personalizes the importance of prayer. A prayer journal is helpful for both listing prayer concerns and also recording the answer to prayers. So often, we remember to pray for an individual but then forget to acknowledge the specific answer to that prayer. Taking the time to reflect on our prayers builds our "prayer muscle" because we see God as a "doer", who responds to our voices when we call out to Him.

On alternate years, we lead a *Home Court Advantage* event on "Devotionals for Early Childhood". Not only do we guide parents in using the excellent material provided by our curriculum, but we also introduce parents to other interesting books and materials created by other Christian publishers, such as the colorful and creative activities from FamiliesAlive. Parents oftentimes want to experience a spiritual connection with their children but they don't know where to start or what to do. Giving them access to this material may be the motivator to parents in engaging in this activity.

First Grade Bible Presentation

At Memorial Park, the First Grade Bible Presentation has become a rite of passage for children. Because they are learning to read in school, the boys and girls look forward to receiving their first "big kid" Bible.

We purchase New International Reader's Version Bibles for all the children on our roles several weeks before the Sunday morning presentation in the church sanctuary. We like this version because it is geared for a third-grade reading level, making it much more understandable for the children. This version includes "helps" sections which bring the Bible to life as children practice their reading skills. Parents can read aloud from the Bible as well, providing a give-and-take exchange between parent and child.

Prior to the presentation, the pastor autographs the Bible for each child, highlighting a special verse just for them. In another church, the parents are asked to highlight a special life verse they have selected for their son or daughter. These verses are then shared with their children on Presentation Sunday. The Children's Ministries leaders purchase and personalize bookmarks for each child, symbolically representing their role in spiritual nurture.

During the actual presentation of Bibles in church, we invite both parents and children to come forward to receive their Bibles. The pastor symbolically stresses the primary role the parents play in the spiritual formation of their children by giving the Bible to the parents. The parents then give the Bible to their children, indicating that it is their responsibility to hand down the Word of God to their own children. Following the presentation in the sanctuary, the parents and children proceed to the classroom. In parent/child groupings they then explore some introductory activities with their new Bibles together. Bible reading plans are also recommended so that the Bibles will be used right away and regularly thereafter. A photographer visits each parent and child, snapping a photo of this important spiritual moment to be given to each family the following week.

At Home Weekly and Homefront Monthly

We enjoy using a curriculum that stresses the importance of living out your faith within the daily rhythms of life. The content of the curriculum makes it easy for parents to engage their children in what they are learning. Excellent articles on marriage, parenting, grandparenting, child development, blessings, craft ideas, and even some delicious, family-friendly recipes entice parents to pick up a copy each month.

Money Matters

Learning how to manage your money is a fundamental skill to be cultivated in the early years of life so that children grow up to be good stewards of all their material possessions as adults. Books such as *Money Matters for Kids* by Larry Burkett and *Your Kids Can Master Their Money* by Ron and Judy Blue and Jeremy White are two excellent resources for the presentation of this topic.

We begin teaching stewardship in elementary school. One Sunday morning a year, we invite parents of children in grades 3-5 to leave the sanctuary so that we can present this material to parents and children together. The pastor has given us his blessing to do so. We share statistics concerning national financial trends and world resources and explain the concepts of tithing, saving, and spending creatively and engagingly.

We use a bin filled with 100 colored plastic balls, like those found in a ball pit, to illustrate this concept. First, we set aside 10 balls to represent our 10% tithe to God. Then we talk about items the children may want for which they need to save. We set aside an appropriate amount for that, approximately 50%. We then discuss ways in which we can use our spending money. Since parents foot the bill for most expenses a child incurs, there isn't a great need for spending money at this age. Therefore, the habits of tithing and saving can be emphasized.

Parents then partner with their son or daughter to compile a list of blessings God has provided them, and discuss practical ways they can put this knowledge into practice right now while still in elementary school. Even though parents hold different philosophies regarding allowances and payment (or non-payment) for chores, most children do have access to some money and they can begin learning responsible habits that can be developed as they grow, take on part-time jobs, and earn money from babysitting, snow-shoveling, and other sporadic work.

Missions, Giving, and Service

Our Children's Ministries staff holds dearly the value of giving to others recognizing that it is never too early for a child to learn generosity, selflessness, and compassion. Therefore, we strive to provide opportunities for children to serve throughout the year. Our focus is "children helping children."

Compassion Day: In the spring, our church holds a Compassion Day, where congregants sign up to undertake various tasks for those in need in our community. The children spend the previous month collecting lunch items such as water, cookies, chips, and fruit, and create greeting cards on Sunday morning during small group time. On Compassion Day, children come with their parents and form assembly lines, making sandwiches for all the Compassion Day volunteers and putting together lunch bags with greeting cards for the rescue mission. We point out to the children that homeless people live just twenty minutes from our home, and so we are caring for our nearby neighbors.

Summer Camp: During our summer camp, we want every child to have lots of fun, develop skills in artistic, culinary, scientific or athletic activities, hear and respond to the gospel in a personal way, and share with others less fortunate! Each year, we choose both a domestic mission organization and an international mission organization to support.

Some local groups we serve include an outreach program housed in a neighboring church and the *Church Army* who runs ministries in an impoverished part of town. We collect household items, food and pantry necessities, and back-to-school supplies; whatever is needed that particular year. We like collecting things such as toilet paper, markers, or canned vegetables because they are tangible items children can appreciate because they need the same things.

We also love supporting EduNations, a ministry founded by our pastor and a few others. EduNations builds schools throughout Sierra Leone, a largely Muslim nation and one of the world's poorest. These schools provide children with a superior education in a Christian environment. Over the years, the campers at *Summer Surge* have provided generators so that each school has power, purchased land and equipment for playgrounds, and sponsored children so that they can go to school. Last year, our campers raised $8,000 in goods and cash to fund these mission projects. They are learning what it means to be generous, selfless, and compassionate!

Sponsorship: The children of MPC have sponsored two children in the last twenty years. We saw our first World Vision child raised to adulthood. We now sponsor an EduNations child, offering a special collection for her on the first Sunday of every month. We have never been without the funds to support these children in all this time.

Christmas Opportunities: In the fall, we love to participate in Operation Christmas Child. With so much attention to what a child wants for Christmas, OCC provides a wonderful opportunity to think of someone else, much less fortunate, who would not otherwise receive any gifts but for the generosity and kindness of strangers. We provide boxes for families in mid-October, encouraging parents to take their children to the store and let them do the shopping, filling up their boxes. The families can then track where their box was sent and include a note, picture, and return address. It's exciting when families receive a return letter from the recipient of their gift!

The children, through their weekly offerings, also support the *Angel Tree Project* of Prison Fellowship, whose mission is to provide gifts to children of incarcerated individuals. We also support our Deacon's Giving Tree, providing gifts to ministries to the homeless, children at risk, international students, families in need, and children of missionaries.

Finally, at our Christmas party in mid-December, the children vote for the projects they most wish to support in the World Vision catalog. Letting children have a say in where their offering money is distributed gives them ownership in this process. No longer do children place money in an offering basket with no idea how the money is spent. They know that every single penny they give goes to missions. Last year, they voted to supply clothes and shoes for children in the United States, life-saving medicines, solar lanterns, ducks, a fishing kit, chickens, a goat, a pig, Bibles, and an insect shield blanket. They also chose to provide a small business loan, a share in a safe home, a share of a hand-drilled well, and to stock a school with supplies. This is what *they* chose, even as elementary age students. They get it!

Over the years, we have produced various Advent activities for families. Most of the ideas were adapted from the book *Redeeming the Season* by Kim Wier and Pam McCune. Some ideas we created for our congregation include Advent Wreaths, The Jesse Tree, Prophecy Boxes, Attribute Ornaments and Gift with Purchase. We assembled all these activities for families so that parents could purchase a kit, open its contents, and keep kids focused on the reason for the season throughout Advent.

Breakout

No! It is not a skin condition! It's an opportunity for kids in grades 4 and 5 to grow in faith. The key to *Breakout* is fun. We start with pizza and sodas, followed by a wide variety of indoor and outdoor games. Then we get serious for a half hour of Bible study, and we finish our time by recording prayer requests in a journal, praying for each other, and reviewing the ways in which God has answered prayers from previous weeks.

In *Breakout*, we focus on discipleship, helping children dig more deeply in their understanding and practice of their faith. We explore the salvation message in greater depth, helping them gain a clearer understanding of sin, salvation, faith, and forgiveness. We also dive into the theology of the Trinity, learn about the sacraments of baptism and communion, and examine aspects of church life such as worship, giving, and fellowship. Character-building and worldview lessons are practically related to everyday life. Children are given practical tools and methods for devotional times and scripture memorization in this series of lessons.

Another key advantage of *Breakout* is the participation of our Middle School coordinator. Children get to build relationships with him even before they transition to Middle School. This relationship also grows during *The Next Big Step*, discussed in the following chapter.

Summer Surge

How can summer camp be a *Home Court Advantage* opportunity for the family? Years ago, we stopped doing Vacation Bible School at our church and started a week-long summer camp we call *Summer Surge*. This captured the spirit of adventure and activity I wanted to infuse in our summer programming. Instead of a pre-packaged formula for VBS, we create our own materials and programming that teach life passages such as the Ten Commandments, the Beatitudes, Psalm 23, the Lord's Prayer, and the Apostle's Creed in depth with real-life applications.

The beauty of camp is the host of activities accompanying the learning that takes place throughout the day, reaching out to all sorts of kids. *Summer Surge* offers basketball, soccer, archery, climbing wall, gymnastics, and street hockey for the athletically-minded; science and programming for the academically-oriented; cooking, baking, crafts, and woodworking for creative individuals; and spa days for those who like to be pampered.

There exists continuity and tradition that builds and sustains children in Summer Surge throughout their growing-up years. Children as young as four years old can register for camp and moms who volunteer receive daycare for their younger children. After three years of Junior Camp, a child can enroll in Day Camp as a first-grader. Four or five years later, this camper is then eligible for Summer Surge Impact, a high-energy adventure camp partially spent on church property and partly on outdoor adventures. As they grow up, former campers join the volunteer team, working as a Junior Counselor at the Junior Camp or as a member of Work Crew. High School students serve as Day Camp Junior Counselors, and college-age students become Day Camp Senior Counselors. Many parents and other caring adults serve in various capacities year after year. Summer Surge gives children a meaningful way to be involved in spiritual formation throughout their childhood, helping them grow and develop their own mature relationship with Jesus Christ.

A Final Word

As always, keep in mind the purpose of this list - not to overwhelm you or make you feel that you must be doing more with your ministry or to follow this blueprint exactly. Instead, the guiding principle is that our ministries will be more effective when we partner with and equip parents to disciple their children. You know the needs of your congregation, your capacity and bandwidth, and what will work in your context.

6

Home Court Advantage: Middle and High School

As students transition into Middle & High School, it continues to be crucial that parents speak into their lives. What follows is a list of *Home Court Advantage* opportunities we provide as a way to equip parents to come alongside their middle & high school-aged children and disciple them.

The Next Big Step

A huge transition for students and parents is the graduation from elementary school into middle school. As any parent can attest, the physical, emotional, social, and academic challenges of kids entering puberty seem daunting, certainly to the kids, but also for parents as they learn to adapt their parenting skills. In fifth grade, most children are blissfully unaware of the seismic shift they are about to experience in the coming months. We want to help parents and tweens prepare for the onset of adolescence, and that is why we created *The Next*

Big Step.

As with *Breakout*, the key to *The Next Big Step* is fun. We design a day-long event for students, their Tru Kids leaders and the Middle School coordinator at a local camp. Getting away to an unfamiliar setting provides a sense of adventure and creates a spirit of togetherness among the participants. We discuss topics such as self-esteem, peer pressure, changing emotions, growing independence, and purpose for our lives.

Initiative games and a low-ropes course are used to reinforce the material we communicate to the students in our three interactive learning sessions. We use the games and the course to draw practical parallels between the physical challenges they experienced and the actual emotional, relational, and spiritual challenges the children will encounter in the next few years.

Meals together, games, and time around the campfire become special relationship-building times. We want the students to know, first and foremost, that we care about them and that they are important members of our group. In years when image and fitting in are so important, we believe the church can be a safe haven for them and a place in which they can invite their friends to know the love and acceptance of others and life-changing love of the Savior.

As the evening concludes, we invite the parents to meet briefly with the leaders of *The Next Big Step*. We share what we have discussed and experienced during the day so that the parents feel included in the experience. We emphasize the importance of continuing dialogue at home and encourage them to purchase a family guide full of tools to advance these discussions with their own son or daughter.

Sixth Grade Bible Presentation

Following up on the important milestone of the First Grade Bible presentation, the Sixth Grade Bible presentation marks another transitional milestone. Now students are no longer dependent upon their parents to read the Bible for or with them. Graduating to a teen Bible provides the tools and insights needed for the next stage of their development.

Our youth leaders present these Bibies to sixth graders on the first week they transition to the youth programs. It serves as a welcome gift, initiating students into the group.

Middle School Stewardship

We address the important subject of stewardship three different times during a child's growing up years. In elementary school, we are simply communicating the concepts of tithing, saving, and spending so that priorities for the use of money can begin to be taught at home.

By the time a child reaches middle school, he or she now has opportunities to earn money through babysitting, lawn mowing, snow shoveling, pet walking, and more. Since this is the first money children manage, we want them to know how to apply these fundamental principles in practical ways. Some parents choose to give their child an allowance, others require their children to begin purchasing some of their own necessities, and others expect their children to pay for their own entertainment.

No matter what position you adopt for your family, the goal remains the same: helping your children use their money in God-honoring, responsible ways.

We use the DVD curriculum *Raising Financially Freed-Up Kids,* in which David Briggs discusses the following:

- Seven keys to preparing your son or daughter to be financially responsible now and in the future

- Creative ways to use allowance as a learning tool for life in the "real world"

- Specific ideas and action steps for kids at each developmental stage—from preschool through high school

- A keen awareness of how healthy financial teaching - and modeling - helps your child build a more solid and joyful life

Middle School Stewardship equips parents to teach their children the cost of food, clothing, gasoline, toiletries, gadgets, cell phone contracts, and other expenses; how to budget for their needs and wants; the patience required to save for a certain expense.

Confirmation

At our church, confirmation is held in the spring of a student's ninth grade year. A confirmation class from September through May leads up to the actual ceremony.

For many families, confirmation is as important as baptism; it serves as a public milestone of a child's faith journey. We choose to stress the importance of the journey itself, regardless of whether or not a student chooses to affiliate with the church upon completion of the course. We are interested in each person expressing true faith and devotion to Jesus Christ. For some children, this occurs in their early years; for others, a faith commitment is not experienced until later in adolescence or adulthood. We want each student to gain a clear understanding of the faith so that they can make a genuine response to Christ whenever they are ready. The confirmation course is an excellent means to that end.

The parents are involved in confirmation by encouraging child's weekly participation in the class, helping their child memorize the Apostles' Creed and the Lord's Prayer at home, and ensuring that their child participates in an area of service within the church. If a person aligns with the church, we want him or her to be an active, contributing participant who experiences a sense of belonging in worship, growth opportunities, and service. We also provide an opportunity in April for parents to attend confirmation class and share their personal walk with Christ with their child. For some families, this is the first time a child may hear his parents verbalize their faith.

Below, I have outlined the scope and sequence of the Confirmation class:

Lesson 1: Why Join the Church?
Lesson 2: The Reliability of the Bible
Lesson 3: Redemptive History: Genesis through Chronicles
Lesson 4: Redemptive History: Poetry, Prophets, Post-Exile
Lesson 5: Redemptive History: New Testament
Lesson 6: Important Creeds: The Ten Commandments
Lesson 7: Important Creeds: The Ten Commandments
Lesson 8: Important Creeds: Westminster Shorter Catechism
Lesson 9: Important Creeds: Apostle's Creed; God the Father
Lesson 10: Important Creeds: Apostle's Creed; God the Son

Lesson 11: Important Creeds: Apostle's Creed; God the Holy Spirit
Lesson 12: Important Creeds: Remainder of the Apostle's Creed
Lesson 13: The Problem of Sin
Lesson 14: Salvation: A Life-Changing Relationship with Jesus Christ (Foreknowledge, Predestination, Calling, Justification)
Lesson 15: Salvation: An Ever-Growing Relationship with Jesus Christ (Adoption, Redemption, Sanctification, Glorification)
Lesson 16: The Lord's Prayer
Lesson 17: The Lord's Prayer
Lesson 18: Sacraments: Baptism
Lesson 19: Sacraments: Baptism
Lesson 20: Sacraments: Communion
Lesson 21: Sacraments: Communion
Lesson 22: S.H.A.P.E. (Spiritual Gifts, Heart, Abilities, Personality, Experience)
Lesson 23: Spiritual Gifts
Lesson 24: Spiritual Gifts
Lesson 25: History and Distinctives of the Denomination
Lesson 26: Church Membership: Worship, Grow, Belong, Serve, Give (Church Member Covenant)
Lesson 27: Parents Share Their Faith with Their Son/Daughter
Lesson 28: Students Write Their Statements of Faith
Lesson 29: Visit from the Pastors/Question and Answer Session

In addition to class time, each student is encouraged to attend youth group and participate in an area of service at church.

Authentic Love

In an age in which abstinence is almost unheard of, it is important to communicate a biblical view of sexuality that is both God-honoring and instills personal worth within young men and women. This message is needed earlier and earlier in a teen's experience because of the sexual innuendo pervading youth culture and the lack of moral, emotional, and social repercussions that arise as a result of sexual activity. Our youth ministry team designed a series called *Authentic Love* to address these issues confronting our teens. Here is the course description:

"Most people want to be in a "relationship": the kind in

which they go out on dates, are shown lots of attention, and are showered with compliments on a daily basis. But even if we don't find ourselves in a romantic relationship, that does not change the fact that we were created to be in relationship with one another. Those relationships include:

- Friendships
- Relationships with Family
- Relationships with God
- Dating/Romantic Relationships
- Marital Relationships

God has created us to be relational beings and He deeply cares about our relationships with each other. But what are God's intentions for our relationships? What does a healthy friendship or dating relationship look like? How do God's intentions differ from our culture's messages regarding relationships? We are going to talk about why relationships matter to God and what it looks like to honor God in every relationship we have or plan to have someday. That includes:

- Friendships (Importance of singleness)
- Dating Relationships (Being "interested" in somebody; "honeymoon phase")
- Romantic Relationships (Purity)
- Marital Relationships (The end goal)

This series is meant for EVERYBODY: not just people who are in dating relationships. God's unconditional love is our focus; it is foundational for any relationship because, only through His love, can we find real or "authentic" love with Him and in other significant relationships in our lives.

Age Group: Middle School and High School (content will be modified for MS and HS respectively).

Curriculum: Various resources (*True Love Waits* curriculum, *Boundaries* by Dr. Henry Cloud and John Townsend, *Every Young Man's Battle* by Stephen Arterburn and Fred Stoeker, among other sources)

Special features: To introduce the series and to provoke interest in the topic, we are asking students to anonymously write down questions they have about relationships (friendships, dating, marriage, etc.) These questions will be discussed during the panel discussion on the final week.

During the "Romantic Relationships" week on purity, we are planning to divide the group according to gender. A female leader will discuss the topic of purity with the girls and a male leader will head the discussion with the guys.

Our final week explores the topic of "Marital Relationships." A panel of people who are in different relationships seasons (one who is single, dating/engaged, recently married, married a while) will field various questions collected at the outset of the program.

We hold a raffle for a free dinner with the youth pastors and their wives for both Middle School and High School, encouraging students to participate in this four-week series. Chances to win will be based on attendance; raffle tickets will be given to every student every week they attend."

It's Not Too Late: Communication is Key

Parents are the primary spiritual influencers of their children, even during the more difficult teen years when they begin to pull away from their parents and peer influences gain ground. Unless a father and mother abdicate their role as parents, the influence they wield is matchless. But lines of communication must remain open, even in the darkest times. When communication is shut down, your teen will seek out other "listening ears" who may or may not have their best interests in mind or at heart. Hearing from seasoned parents who have negotiated these "waters" already can bring current parents of teens hope and wise counsel with the specific dilemmas they face.

Dan Dupee is the chairman of the board of the Coalition for Christian Outreach, a campus ministry working annually with over 32,000 students on over 115 campuses. He and his wife, Carol, are the parents of four grown children. He is the author of the book It's Not Too Late, describing the essential part parents play in shaping their teen's faith. Our church hosts an event in which Dan is invited to present his compelling message to parents from our community churches, giving them the motivation and the tools to continue this important work of spiritual formation through their teen years.

Senior High Stewardship

As high school juniors, many are obtaining their learner's permits and practicing driving skills. A driver's license signifies growing independence and responsibility, as well as lessening the role of chauffeur on the part of mom or dad. Students are preparing for SATs, applying to college, or making plans for post-high school employment.

Saving for the future becomes a present reality; saving for school, for a car, for an apartment, and more. Yet the same principles learned in elementary school still apply; tithing, saving, and spending. Learning to live within one's means, not relying on credit, and budgeting prepare a student for future responsibilities. These concepts are most effectively taught at home through the practical experiences parents have encountered along the way. Both good practices, as well as financial regrets, can be huge life lessons and cautionary tales.

Generation Change, written by Dave Ramsey and Rachel Cruze, is a nine-session, video-based curriculum that teaches students the following:

- Be Who God Created You to Be: "Once you figure out who you really are and what you actually care about, it's easy to be who God created you to be. Our identity is not wrapped up in what the world says about you; your identity is in Christ."

- Do More with Your Money: "To do more with your money, you've got to manage it well." Budgeting is discussed in depth in this section. Because we are stewards of all that belongs to God, we need to manage well that which has been entrusted to us.

- Go Write Your Story: "If you follow God's way of handling money, you really can live a debt-free life." Topics include building a resume and preparing for an interview. The importance of insurance and investing is also discussed.

Family Forums

The desire to establish *Family Forums* arose from focus groups I hosted while researching for this book. When asked about the hot topics facing families today, many people expressed the desire to continue the conversation with others. Sometimes we can feel isolated or overwhelmed by the issues we are confronting. It is important to know that you are not alone; others share your convictions and are interested in discussing solutions and responses that are life-giving and God-honoring.

Our goal is to be on the cutting edge, offering parents relevant, realistic responses to life matters that most concern them. These forums extend beyond the church family and into the larger community as well. They may point others to spiritual truths and values they had not previously considered.

Quarterly *Family Forums* provide opportunities for experts in their fields to present information to parents, enabling them to engage their sons and daughters in meaningful conversation. Some of our hot topics include a discussion on smart cell phone usage for middle schoolers; a gender identity talk for parents so they can discuss this highly-charged topic sensitively with their teens; a discussion on depression, anxiety, and suicide among teenagers, a presentation on the opioid crisis and other forms of substance abuse; as well as other topics such as sex-trafficking, racism and reconciliation, the assault of social media and its effects on kids today; and the value of honesty and integrity as it relates to academics and success in life.

Baccalaureate

High School graduation marks the most significant milestone in a child's first eighteen years of life. Family members gather from near and far to celebrate this huge accomplishment as they anticipate the next chapter of life soon to begin. The church can play a significant role in honoring each graduate and their parents.

We ask parents to write a letter to their son or daughter in May of their senior year. We ask them to reflect upon the ways their hopes and dreams for their child, written at the time of their child's baptism, have been realized. We encourage them to share ways in which they have witnessed the Lord at work in and through their child in their growing up years and to share new hopes and dreams for their child's future.

In this same time period, we ask all graduating seniors to write a letter to their parents, giving thanks to them for all the sacrifices they have made, for the examples they have been, and for the lessons they have learned from them. We encourage them to share how the Lord has impacted their lives, and the specific lessons they have learned.

We celebrate Baccalaureate at our church one Sunday in early June. We create a short biography of each student for our worship bulletin. High school graduates, youth leaders, and parents all participate in the service in some way, whether that is by leading worship, sharing testimonies, reading Scripture, or participating vocally or instrumentally. At that time, the exchange of letters occurs between parents and students; powerful moments indeed. We give each student a copy of *Oh, The Places You'll Go!*, by Dr. Suess, signed by the parents, siblings, pastors, and youth leaders, along with a frameable copy of Joshua 1:9. Prayer partners from the congregation are assigned to each graduate for one year; these partners can choose to recommit on an annual basis. We desire this service to be a bookend service to the baptism service the family experienced eighteen years earlier.

The Importance of the Church

As we conclude our look at the *Home Court Advantage* blueprint, I cannot over-emphasize the need for the church to incorporate and value its children, not just for discipleship, but for their continued involvement in the church. Jim Burns, president of HomeWord, says this best: "The children in your church need to know that they aren't the future of the church but rather their involvement matters right now. When kids feel empowered to be integrated into the life of the church, they will stay. If they feel only like spectators, they eventually leave." What we do with our children right now, every week, makes an impact, not only for the present time but also for the future.

7

What the Family Can Do

I'm the proud owner of a Sunday School Perfect Attendance pin for twelve years running. I earned this honor back in the 1960s when church attendance in the United States was much different than today. My parents began sending my brothers, sister and me to Sunday School at age 2, and I never missed a Sunday in my entire young life. My father would drop us off at the church or, in good weather, we walked there on our own. My parents attended church once each year, and that was on Easter Sunday.

Even when we went on vacation, my parents made sure my siblings and I attended Sunday School so that we could get credit for our attendance. Imagine walking alone into an unfamiliar church filled with strangers; it was definitely a dreaded experience. I had heard Bible stories countless times; I could recite verses and name the books of the Bible in order in record time. But there was one tiny problem… I didn't believe any of it.

As I entered adolescence, I described myself as a deist. I did believe in a spiritual being who created the universe. I just didn't believe He could be known as my Sunday School teachers taught. Miracles had no place in my reasoning; I was becoming a product of the culture around me instead of a transformed person impacting the prevailing culture for Christ. When I look back on my lack of faith formation, I'm intrigued as to why the faith didn't stick to me. Why were others able to believe and accept what they heard, but it fell flat when it came to me?

Only later in life did it dawn on me. I didn't believe because my parents didn't believe, either. They sent us to Sunday School because it was the socially acceptable thing to do, but they never went. Apart from a rote grace at dinnertime or a recited bedtime prayer, Christianity played no role in our family; the faith was completely irrelevant to the rest of daily life. Santa Claus had as much chance of being real as did Jesus Christ.

What is the point of this story? If we want to raise the next generation to know, love, and serve the Lord Jesus Christ, we need to engage parents as the primary spiritual influencers of their children. They are the ones who will pass down a vibrant, relevant faith to their children through the example they set for them, utilizing the resources and guidance the church can provide. Instead of relying on the church to impact the next generation spiritually in just one hour each week, we need to enable parents to impact their own children one hundred sixty-eight hours each week.

This is the paradigm shift that must take place for families in today's culture, awakening transforming faith in Jesus Christ by being relationally relevant to parents and children from the outset, providing real leadership and encouragement to families, with easy-to-incorporate ideas that can be experienced in the natural rhythm and flow of daily life.

In 2003, George Barna wrote an amazing book that raises the value of children and the need for the church to come alongside families, equipping parents to do the hard work of parenting in an increasingly hostile culture. *Transforming Children into Spiritual Champions* awakens us to the needs of children which must be responsibly addressed if the faith is to be passed down to the next generation. Here are some of the insights he gained as a result of his research.

Focusing on children age 5-12, he raises this question, "Why focus on this particular slice of the youth market? Because if you want to shape a person's life—whether you are most concerned about his or her moral, spiritual, physical, intellectual, emotional or economic development—it is during these crucial eight years that lifelong habits, values, beliefs and attitudes are formed."[1]

Barna goes on to say:

"Nine out of 10 young people (93 percent) consider themselves to be Christian by age 13. For a large portion of those kids, however, being Christian does not correspond to having a grace-based personal relationship with Jesus Christ; and for a large share of the self-professed Christians, commitment to that faith is minimal.

Among those who say they are Christian, only 35 percent indicate that they are "absolutely committed to the Christian faith." A majority, 54 percent, say they are "moderately committed," while the remaining 10 percent says they are not committed to Christianity.

A different way of assessing the faith commitment of young people is to determine whether they are evangelical, born again, nominal Christian, aligned with a non-Christian faith, or an atheist or agnostic. If born-again Christians are described as those who say they have made an important personal commitment to Jesus Christ and who believe they will have eternal life solely because they have confessed their sins and accepted Jesus Christ as their Savior, then we estimate that 34 percent of children are born again by age 13.

A subset of the born-again segment are the evangelicals. These individuals are not only born again but also have a belief system that is more strongly aligned with biblical teachings in specific areas. Evangelicals would strongly affirm the accuracy of all biblical teachings, the personal responsibility to share their faith in Christ with non-believers, the centrality of faith in a person's life, the inability to attain eternal salvation except through the grace of God through Jesus Christ's death and resurrection, the nature of God as

---

1   George Barna, *Transforming Children into Spiritual Champions* (Ventura, CA: Regal Books, 2003), p. 18.

the creator and sustainer of all that exists, and the existence of Satan (God's enemy) as a real being, not merely a symbol of evil. Using this approach, just 4 percent of all 13-year-olds are "notional Christians"—people who say they are Christian but are not committed followers of Christ in any discernible way."[2]

About evangelism, Barna notes that "a series of studies we conducted regarding the age at which people accept Christ as their Savior highlights the importance of having people invite Jesus into their heart as their Savior when they are young. We discovered that the probability of someone embracing Jesus as his or her Savior was 32 percent for those between the ages of 5 and 12; 4 percent for those in the 13- to 18-age range; and 6 percent for people 19 or older. In other words, if people do not embrace Jesus Christ as their Savior before they reach their teenage years, the chance of their doing so at all is slim."[3]

And even more indicative: "By the age of nine, most of the moral and spiritual foundations of a child are in place."[4]

Typically, congregations invest lots of time and money in reaching the adult population in their churches and communities. But if 32% of those coming to faith in Christ make that decision before age 12, where should resources be allocated? If chances are slim that an individual will make a commitment to Christ after age 19, how invested should we be in regard to children and teens in both high school and college? Providing vibrant, captivating ministries to children and youth is one of the most engaging pathways for reaching parents with the gospel and equipping them to impact their own children at home.

---

2   George Barna, *Transforming Children into Spiritual Champions* (Ventura, CA: Regal Books, 2003), p. 33.

3   George Barna, *Transforming Children into Spiritual Champions* (Ventura, CA: Regal Books, 2003), p. 34.

4   George Barna, *Transforming Children into Spiritual Champions* (Ventura, CA: Regal Books, 2003), p. 58.

Factors Working Against the Family

One of the greatest myths regarding parenting is that parents become increasingly peripheral in the lives of their growing children. This belief oftentimes becomes a self-fulfilling prophecy. Parents think their influence is waning and they tend to retreat, lessening the positive impact they could continue to wield with their own son or daughter. In his excellent book *It's Never Too Late*, Dan Dupee cites the work of Notre Dame professor and researcher Christian Smith. In seeking to understand the spiritual lives of young people he discovered a few factors evident in those with an active faith, which are:

1. The influence and example of highly religious parents.

2. The high importance of religious faith for a teen.

3. The teen has many religious experiences.

4. The teen frequently prays and reads Scripture.

5. The teen has many adults in a congregation to turn to for help and support.

6. The teen has few or no doubts about religious belief.[5]

Dupee goes on to share the specifics of what young people need for success. Note how many have to do with their families:

"Search Institute has identified 40 positive supports and strengths that young people need to succeed. Half of the assets focus on the relationships and opportunities they need in their families, schools, and communities (external assets). The remaining assets focus on the social-emotional strengths, values, and commitments that are nurtured within young people (internal assets).

The assets can be grouped as follows:

Support: Young people need to be surrounded by people who love, care for, appreciate, and accept them.

---

5   Dan Dupee, It's Not Too Late (Grand Rapids, MI: Baker Books, 2016), p. 63.

Empowerment: Young people need to feel valued and valuable. This happens when youth feel safe and respected.

Boundaries and Expectations: Young people need clear rules, consistent consequences for breaking rules, and encouragement to do their best.

Constructive Use of Time: Young people need opportunities—outside of school—to learn and develop new skills and interests with other youth and adults.

Commitment to Learning: Young people need a sense of the lasting importance of learning and a belief in their own abilities.

Positive Values: Young people need to develop strong guiding values or principles to help them make healthy life choices.

Social Competencies: Young people need the skills to interact effectively with others, to make difficult decisions, and to cope with new situations.

Positive Identity: Young people need to believe in their own self-worth and to feel that they have control over the things that happen to them."[6]

The research is clear - overwhelmingly, the most important influencers of children are their mother and father. The sad truth is that many parents have abdicated their spiritual influence and responsibility to the church. With spotty attendance, that influence may yield less than four hours per month. Much of that time is spent in large group activities or teaching rather than one-on-one conversations dealing with the relevance and application of these spiritual truths into daily life.

Parents have many reasons for abdicating their roles. Some find communication with their child difficult, especially as they reach their teenage years. They sometimes think the youth minister is more skilled in relating to their child than they are. They would rather leave some of the more difficult discussions to the "experts."

---

6   Search Institute, The Developmental Assets Framework, 1997.

Other parents feel ill-equipped in fostering their child's faith. They may or may not have been raised in the church or remember anything they may have been taught. Because they don't know how to pray or read the Bible devotionally, they have no idea how to initiate these practices with their own children. Barna discovered "that in a typical week, fewer than 10 percent of parents who regularly attend church with their kids read the Bible together, pray together (other than at meal times) or participate in an act of service as a family unit. Even fewer families—1 out of every 20—have any type of worship experience together with their kids, other than while they are at church during a typical month."[7]

Parents permit secular sources to influence their children, often without many filters in place. Barna remarks, "Did you catch the notion that what you allow your child to ingest from mass media—movies, television, music, books and the Internet, in particular—probably has more cumulative impact than what you try to teach, thus making your role as the gatekeeper for media exposure enormously significant?"[8]

Competition with other activities is winning the "time war." When unrealistic demands from extracurricular activities and homework impact our children, there is little free time left for anything else. Children can skip church or even private devotions because they aren't going to be graded and they didn't have to pay for these activities. Parents are more committed to hockey or soccer because they paid for their child to participate in the league. Church happens when nothing else interferes.

A final factor working against the family has to do with perception. Many people find the church irrelevant; they don't think of the church as a place or as a group of people who can help them "do life" with their son or daughter. Parents tune into pop psychologists, authors of books found in the grocery aisle, sports figures, teachers, TV celebrities, and other family members to sort through the problems they face. They fail to

---

7   George Barna, *Transforming Children into Spiritual Champions* (Ventura, CA: Regal Books, 2003), p. 78.

8   George Barna, *Transforming Children into Spiritual Champions* (Ventura, CA: Regal Books, 2003), p. 60.

consider that the God who created them and loves them also knows exactly how to address the issues confronting them.

Despite all the many ways parents have abdicated their spiritual responsibilities to their children, Barna's research reveals key contradictions in parents' thinking:

- "Even though only 5 percent of churched parents have a biblical worldview, two-thirds (64 percent) of all churched parents think they are doing an excellent or good job of helping their children to develop a worldview based on the Bible.

- Although fewer than 10 percent of churched households spend any time at all during a typical week either reading the Bible or engaging in substantive prayer as a family unit, about 3 out of every 4 (72 percent) churched parents believe they are doing well when it comes to providing a regular regimen of spiritual experiences and instruction to their children.

- Despite the fact that fewer than one-twentieth of churched households ever worship God outside of a church service or have any type of regular Bible study or devotional time together during a typical week and that almost two-thirds of the children of church families are not born again, three-fourths (72 percent) of those parents claim they are doing a stellar job of nurturing their children's relationship with God."[9]

Dan Dupee comments, "For many Christian kids, their faith is not a way of life but an extracurricular activity or like a hobby. This is the model they observe in their families. My point here is not necessarily that we need to raise the bar for our kids, though we do, but that we need to expect more from ourselves. We need to be intentionally influential in the lives of kids in our church community. We need to invite adults from that community to be influential in the lives of our kids."[10]

---

9   George Barna, *Transforming Children into Spiritual Champions* (Ventura, CA: Regal Books, 2003), p. 125.

10   Dan Dupee, It's Not Too Late (Grand Rapids, MI: Baker Books, 2016), p. 119.

Parents must awaken to the critical role they play in shaping the spiritual lives of their children, beginning at birth. They must face the fact that their family's misplaced priorities are contributing to the neglect of their child's spiritual formation and subsequent world view, and ultimately, the shirking off of faith by their sons and daughters as they reach young adulthood.

If faith is reduced to moralistic teaching and good behavior, then we have severely gone off course. If faith is understanding how to live out the deepest convictions of our hearts by the power of God's Holy Spirit, then it can only be experienced day by day and through the most significant relationships in our lives. Mark Holmen, the founder and executive director of Faith@Home Ministries says, "If we simply did a better job discipling our own children in our homes, not only would we end the decline of Christianity in America, but it would become the fastest-growing religion."[11]

The Changing Paradigm

Jim Burns, president of HomeWord, succinctly states, "One of the purposes of the church is to mentor parents; the parents mentor their children, and the legacy of faith continues to the next generation." The church of the latter twentieth century was a full-service operation for the raising of our youth. Until very recently, well-meaning volunteers and a few paid staff people were largely responsible for the spiritual well-being of our children. We called these individuals "shepherds" and placed our children in small groups under their tutelage.

Even though we are indebted to these individuals for their spiritual service, we now realize that they cannot be the primary spiritual influencers of our child if he or she is really going to catch the faith and make it her own. Equipping and discipling parents so they possess the tools they need to fulfill this huge spiritual responsibility is key.

In Deuteronomy 6:4-9 we read the following, "Hear, O Israel: the LORD our God, the LORD is one. Love the LORD your God with all your heart and with all your soul and with all your

---

11   Mark Holmen, Faith@Home Ministries.

strength. These commandments that I give you today are to be upon your hearts. Impress them on your children. Talk about them when you sit at home and when you walk along the road, when you lie down and when you get up. Tie them as symbols on your hands and bind them on your foreheads. Write them on the doorframes of your houses and on your gates."

This spiritual equipping is not a church program. It is an interpersonal experience of daily life. We share with our children what the Lord is teaching us; the truths He is imprinting in our own hearts. Children can be taught the faith, but it is best "caught" when they experience it in real time and in real life. Again, this passage does not suggest a certain time or place in which we impress spiritual truths on our children. Rather, the Scripture suggests that it is discussed at home, in the car, or walking on the road: all activities within the ebb and flow of daily life. Much like the Family Mission Statement we discussed, we are to write these commandments on the doorframes of our house. We proclaim to others who we are in Christ as a family, and who we seek to serve.

Psalm 78:1-7 provides additional insights for our parental responsibilities.

"O my people, hear my teaching; listen to the words of my mouth. I will open my mouth in parables, I will utter things hidden from of old—things we have heard and known, things our fathers have told us. We will not hide them from their children; we will tell the next generation the praiseworthy deeds of the LORD, his power, and the wonders he has done. He decreed statutes for Jacob and established the law in Israel, which he commanded our forefathers to teach their children, so the next generation would know them, even the children yet to be born, and they in turn would tell their children. Then they would put their trust in God and would not forget his deeds but would keep his commands."

Notice that we are encouraged to tell our children about the wonders God has done. We are to speak about the things we know from our own experience as well as the stories we have heard from others. Children, as well as their parents, need to see God as a "doer." His deeds are praiseworthy, and therefore, He is worthy of praise. He is our champion, in whom we can put our confident trust. He is real, and He impacts our personal lives and those of every living creature; He is not a theory, an idea, or an ephemeral spirit.

God has not left us alone to solve all parenting issues through our own wisdom. He has provided the faith community to come alongside us in this awesome responsibility. As Dan Dupee remarks, "Your kids need models of healthy families and diverse individuals. They need other believing adults to connect with them in ways you cannot. . . . It lends power and credibility to the gospel message when your children see it embraced by people for whom they have affection and respect and who they know are genuinely interested not only in Jesus but in them."[12]

Changes Within a Generation

We are all acquainted with the seven deadly words: "It has always been done this way." A similar sentiment states, "It never has been done this way." On the contrary, I would encourage you to think of the changes that have come about in our lifetime. When I was a child, we drove to Florida for a family vacation in our family sedan; three in the front and three in the back on bench seats. There were no seat belts; my siblings and I sprawled over the back seat. The youngest child got to sit with mom and dad in the front seat. Today we have child restraints for children through elementary school, and the wearing of seat belts is law. We are appalled at those not taking those measures to ensure their child's safety.

When I was a teenager, my sister and I loved to sunbathe using baby oil with a splash of iodine to enhance color. We would never fry our bodies in that same way today. Thousands of other sun worshippers pay the price today for the vanity of their youth in the form of skin cancer and aging skin. Dermatologists have an unending supply of patients to treat. What were we thinking?

In today's present climate, we are much more environmentally friendly than a generation ago. When I was a child, the term

---

12   Dan Dupee, It's Not Too Late (Grand Rapids, MI: Baker Books, 2016), pp. 109-110.

"recycling" was largely unknown. Absolutely everything went into the trash can; we disposed of things with abandon. Today we can recycle glass, paper, metals, and compost food products, leaves, and other organic matter. We exercise care in the disposal of chemicals and are careful to treat wastewater. We have gained a new level of understanding and commitment to the protection of our environment, not only for ourselves but for future generations.

We have readily incorporated those changes into our lifestyles within just one generation; we can just as easily infuse our spiritual lives with some alterations that can make a global impact for our individual families and churches.

Someone else once said the definition of insanity is doing the same thing over and over, anticipating a different result. During a seminar I led, one man questioned the efficacy of one of the initiatives I suggested. He wanted statistics to prove this idea had validity. He had a good point; we don't want to waste our time pursuing ineffective ideas. But we have got to start somewhere. We can't do *nothing*. We have to try *something* and then adapt, alter, develop or scrap the idea if it is unworkable. We need to stop doing some things and start doing other things because what we are currently doing is, in part, causing us to lose the next generation for Christ.

As the Serenity Prayer states, "God grant me the serenity to accept the things I cannot change, courage to change the things I can, and the wisdom to know the difference." Let us be people that pursue needed change courageously.

8

Living Your Faith with Your Family

Creating Traditions

When you think back to your own childhood, you can probably remember, season by season, certain distinctives about your family that made your family unique. You may remember snow days spent sledding followed by hot chocolate around the fire, special Valentine's boxes and treats, visits by the tooth fairy, Easter Egg hunts, birthday parties, special family dinners, rewards for good report cards, family vacations, back-to-school traditions, harvest activities, Thanksgiving and Christmas. There is so much to celebrate if we put a little effort into making these times special. But we don't need to wait for a holiday to create a tradition. Many activities, such as prayer or devotions, become the hallmarks that distinguish our family from others and bond us with our children.

However, many people come from families who didn't purposefully create these memories during childhood. For those individuals, it's never too early to begin your own traditions!

You have the privilege of deciding how you will celebrate each holiday, and how you can infuse meaning into daily and annual activities on your calendar.

Some holidays we observe and activities we participate in are just for fun. For instance, there is no particular spiritual significance to the Tooth Fairy. Other activities have the potential to instill life-long values and spiritual truth into our children's lives. Both types of activities make our families unique and special and are worth investing in.

I recently conducted an informal survey to round up a variety of family traditions, and I have included the results below. The ideas that follow are not exhaustive but are meant to jump-start your own creativity in establishing some family practices that your children can anticipate year after year. All the ideas are organized chronologically by season.

David Baer, Executive Director at FamiliesAlive, once commented that "many families excel at creating fun traditions with their families, but don't know where to start faith-based traditions. If we are being intentional about passing the faith to our children, our traditions should reflect this. '' Thus, in addition to the survey results, I have included some meaningful tradition ideas from FamiliesAlive and other sources that are meant to equip parents to intentionally live out their faith at home.

New Year's Day

Although it can become cliché, many folks use January 1 as a day to begin New Year's resolutions. For most people, the resolution has to do with losing weight. But many other resolutions can be attempted, such as committing to read the Bible in a year or pray every day. Holding another family member accountable in this practice or participating with your child in this activity is a great way to bond spiritually.

Valentine's Day

Valentine's Day is a great opportunity to express love to your children. Many parents cited the assembly of the Valentine's Day box for school as an example of a fun family project. Little candy hearts with sentiments are fun ways to share your affection for others.

Several women mentioned a little gift or treat their parents, particularly their fathers, gave them on this holiday. One woman said that, although she was now 43 years old, her parents still presented her with a small gift each year. I still have a piece of costume jewelry my father gave me when I was a young girl. It is a gold-sprayed Cupid perched upon a beautiful lavender ball. I remember thinking that it was the most beautiful piece of jewelry I owned as a child, and it is safely kept in my jewelry box today. Moms could remember their sons in similar ways.

One way to emphasize familial love is to participate in activities deliberately designed to make each family member feel special. Ask each family member "what makes you feel loved?" Perhaps mom feels loved when the family chips in - give her a night off and have the rest of the family cook, set the table, and clean up one night. Perhaps little brother feels loved when he gets to play his favorite sport - have everyone go to the park and play soccer together!

Valentine's Day is an excellent time to reflect on the reason we love others - because God first loved us. Read 1 John 4:7-21 as a family and discuss together.

Easter

Many folks mentioned Easter sunrise services with their families as important memories of Easter. One woman mentioned that she would take her daughter to that early service as a remembrance of the women who went to the tomb early that first resurrection morning, discovering that Jesus had risen from the dead. Another family went to McDonald's for breakfast following the service!

Basket-hunting, egg-dyeing, egg hunts, and family dinners were enjoyed by many families. One parent got creative and had her children follow a trail of yarn throughout the house that led to their Easter baskets. One year, my family was visiting my husband's parents in Florida, who owned a lovely home with a pool on their lanai. I stuffed plastic eggs with candy and other treats and tossed them into the pool for an Easter egg dive! That was hugely entertaining for everyone.

A great way to engage even small children with the Easter Story is to use the Resurrection Eggs from FamilyLife. These eggs are filled with small items that represent part of the Easter story, like a mini crown of thorns or a donkey figurine. Let children open the eggs, discover the symbol, and re-tell that portion of the Easter story!

For older children, allow them to engage creatively with the Easter story. Perhaps assign a portion of the Scriptures for them to read or discuss, or give them a prompt, such as "which character of Jesus' death and resurrection do you most identify with?". Then, share together as a group.

School Events

Most people cited rewards for good report cards as a favorite memory; gifts ranging from pizza to baseball cards! Back-to-school shopping, a special school-eve dinner, and first-day-of-school pictures create anticipation for the coming year and remind us how our children have grown throughout the years. One mom hosted an afternoon tea for her daughter following the first day of school in order to hear about her day. Children learn what is important to their parents by watching what they do and the emphasis they place on certain activities.

Consider hosting a back-to-school dinner with a few other family friends. You can use this to celebrate the occasion, and also to pray over kids before they start at school.

Vacations

Most of us remember random events in our childhood as much as we remember big events. Our experiences influence how we choose to spend our leisure time with our own families. Many families opt for the same beach vacation at the same locale year after year. The rental house expands as the family grows. Others choose a hybrid version of vacation, mixing learning with pleasure, such as visiting both the historic sites of Boston before relaxing at Cape Cod.

Our family chose to go on "great adventures" to National Parks throughout the country, hoping to inspire and educate our children to the great wonders that existed outside our community. We were able to visit 21 parks and all four corners of the United States. Our children learned to love the outdoors, hiking, kayaking, biking, and growing in their appreciation for

God's beautiful creation.

We certainly did have a few misfires in our treks. I remember the time my children refused to go into the stinky Great Salt Lake, the seemingly endless drive through the desert to Dinosaur National Monument, and days when all we saw was a bunch of rocks, according to my six-year-old daughter. But through these misfires, we also experienced the crater of a volcano, waterfalls, the calving of glaciers, rain forests, sliding down snowy Mt. Rainier on our backsides, panning for gold in Montana, encountering moose in the wilderness, hiking to awesome vistas and much, much more. Those trips, carefully crafted, have become special memories for us all.

Harvest Activities

From harvest parties at church to pumpkin-carving, trick-or-treating, and candy exchanges, October is a great time for hayrides, hot cider, and s'mores at a fire pit. One woman recalls going on "leaf drives" on Sundays with Grandma to see the changing fall colors. Somehow, they always found the best places to eat!

Halloween can be tricky for Christian families to navigate. Some may choose to participate while others boycott the holiday entirely. What is important is that parents prayerfully take this decision to Jesus and intentionally try to honor Him with what they choose to do.

One idea for redeeming the holiday is to hold a canned-food drive on the one night of the year when people expect you to knock on their doors! The Shultz family has been doing this for almost a decade. They pass out flyers a week in advance, and then on Halloween night, they get together a bunch of families, eat chili, and head out to the neighborhood to collect non-perishable food items (and candy, of course). The next day, they bring it all to the local Rescue Mission.

Thanksgiving

Thanksgiving traditions center on two primary themes, food and family. This feast, with turkey as the centerpiece, is concocted in a variety of ways. Grandma, mom, dad, or a favorite aunt are the usual chefs, with a variety of sides from sweet potatoes to pumpkin pie. Board games, hide-and-seek, or college football games generally follow dinner, providing a little friendly competition and lots of laughter as everyone interacts.

A meaningful tradition is to have each person share a variety of things they are thankful for. These can be off-the-cuff or written ahead of time and collected to reflect upon in the future. It is also a great opportunity to express gratitude for your Lord and Savior, and perhaps mom or dad can lead the family in a toast before dinner to everything God has done.

Christmas

A friend of mine once remarked that she had no Christmas traditions. She had grown up in a home in which faith did not exist and thus there was no spiritual or secular observance of the holiday. I suggested that this experience was her opportunity to establish some traditions of her own, some activities that would uniquely become a part of her family's life together.

More traditions surround Christmas than any other holiday. Throughout Advent, activities including adorning the house with lights, decorating the Christmas tree, hanging stockings by the fireplace, baking everyone's favorite cookies, sending and receiving Christmas greetings fill the days with anticipation.

On Christmas Eve, many families attend church together followed by holiday snacking and favorite Christmas movies such as "The Muppet Christmas Carol," "The Polar Express," or "It's a Wonderful Life". Some families read the Christmas Story; others participate in the church's live nativity.

Christmas day arrives, with presents to unwrap and cinnamon buns to be eaten. Each family has its own gift-unwrapping protocol: youngest to oldest; stockings first; stockings last; one at a time and around the circle. Families gather for Christmas dinner and for visits throughout the year's end.

The entire season of Advent is a great time to celebrate Jesus' birth, no matter how old your children are. Young children may enjoy making paper chains and cutting off a link each day and announcing the number of days until Christmas. There are a variety of advent devotionals that you can use to guide your family in intentional worship leading up to Christmas.

In the week leading up to Christmas, the Shultz family reads Bible passages together about Jesus being the light of the world, then goes out on a drive to look at Christmas lights. This is another way to center yourselves on the true meaning of Christmas.

One tradition based on the gifts the Magi brought to Jesus involves avoiding materialism by only buying three gifts per child - a want, a need, and a spiritual gift. This is a good way to remember why we give gifts to each other (because Jesus is the greatest gift of all!)

New Year's Eve

Staying up until midnight to watch the ball drop is the most fun for children after snacking, playing games, and even feasting at a chocolate fountain. Football is the main focus for some families on New Year's Day; others, especially those of German heritage anticipate a traditional pork and sauerkraut dinner.

New Year's Eve also provides a great opportunity to look back with gratitude on the previous year. Have each person in the family name something great that happened or a prayer that was answered, and be sure to thank God for all He has done in your family!

Birthdays

Birthdays are great opportunities for family gatherings and parties with friends. Many families give the birthday boy and girl their choice of restaurants or meals to be served on a special plate by mom or dad.

Birthday cakes are integral to a birthday celebration. In our home, my mom would bake a sheet cake each year and decorate it with circus animals. This was a big hit with friends until the day the circus animals were set afire and the blaze consumed the cake. That ended the years of circus cakes, but what a spectacular end it was.

My mom then resorted to purchasing layer cakes with the birthday person's name inscribed with frosting on the top of the cake. Wanting to record this event pictorially, my mother photographed the cake as it was tilted, ever so gently, so the writing could be read. My grandmother, over-eager to help, managed to flip the entire cake upside down and into a glass of milk. I don't recall any cakes after that particular birthday celebration.

Birthdays are lovely ways to remember the specialness of someone, no matter how it is recognized. Even adults, who don't want to discuss their specific age love the expression of being remembered and cherished one day each year.

Perhaps you can gather as a family to share memories of the birthday boy or girl. Have each person share a story, a funny memory, or a reason they are thankful for that family member. Then, pray to the Lord, thanking him for the gift of the birthday person to your family.

Sundays

Most families I surveyed didn't have any specific Sunday traditions or ways to keep Sunday special. In bygone days, families made church attendance part of their Sunday routine. As families get busier and busier, the value placed upon worship has disintegrated. We now consider two out of four Sundays to be "regular" attendance and yet our children rarely miss a sports practice; our values have been skewed.

Growing up, our pastor's family emphasized REST on Sundays. Afternoon naps were encouraged; no sports were played, no friends visited. Dinner was simple. Today, our pastor's daughter practices the Sabbath similarly with her own family. She has found this day to be life-giving and restoring in her busy life as a wife, mother, and co-worker in ministry.

Growing up, my mother never cooked on Sunday, so we either had chicken noodle soup or they would spring for Chinese take-out. We mostly thought Sundays were boring, particularly when the family went for a Sunday drive. We don't take a ride in the car any longer, but we do look forward to a slower pace on Sunday afternoons.

One simple way to rest on Sundays is to unplug. One pastor's family recently got into the habit of turning off their phones at least one hour every day, one day every week, and one week every year. The dedicated "no screens" day each week is Sunday, and it has been a great way for them to remember the Sabbath together.

Tooth Fairy

The Tooth Fairy operates differently, depending upon where you reside. Some children receive a mere $0.25 while others net up to $5 per tooth. Sometimes the Tooth Fairy leaves notes or puts your cash in a special pillow.

At my house, the Tooth Fairy often forgot to show up the night before, so after my son or daughter left their bedroom, the Tooth Fairy would deliver a gift buried somewhere in their sheets and blankets instead of under the pillow. Sometimes, they just didn't look hard enough, I told them.

Other Days

Some of our fondest memories from childhood involve play, including snow days of sledding and hot chocolate. Other important summer celebrations included neighborhood picnics on Memorial Day, the Fourth of July, and Labor Day. These potluck dinners, in which everyone brought their specialty, involved neighbors and relatives from far and near.

Another terrific tradition is involving the whole family in household tasks. In my home, mowing the lawn, trimming, and edging on Saturday morning were most efficiently completed with everyone involved. Fall provided us with plenty of leaves to rake, and winter gave us lots of snow to shovel. When the work was done, play began. There is value to sharing in the responsibilities of taking care of our own home with our children.

Everyday Activities

Utilizing the resources provided by our church, we are able to advance the spiritual formation of our children on a daily basis, beginning at birth.

Music

Music can be soothing, playful, fun, energizing, thought-provoking or reflective. From the first moments of our children's lives, we played Christian lullabies during the wee hours of the morning during those nighttime feedings. Singing beautiful, truth-filled lyrics to them began the process of instilling God's love in them. These moments inspired the "Welcome to Our World" CD our church presents to all parents of newborns.

Selecting uplifting music is critical for all ages; it often sets the mood for our days and influences our perspectives in life. It can be employed to conform ourselves to the culture around us or to Christ. Thankfully, there are lots of Christian artists and genres of music from which to choose.

Stories

Children love stories, and enjoy cuddling with their parents; it is a great bonding experience for everyone! We built storytime into our bedtime routines for many years, beginning in the first year of life all the way through elementary school. Staying up just a little bit longer for one more story made the children think they were getting away with not going to bed, but we knew this plan was totally intentional. We read from a Bible storybook to conclude our story time each evening, beginning the habit of daily Bible reading with our family.

This motivated us to purchase story Bibles for the *My First Bible* activity at church. It further compelled us to discover other Christian storybooks appropriate for spiritual formation in young children and to share them with parents of children in that age group. Sometimes, our Sunday morning curriculum provides ideas for families to do together during the week. Those devotions coincide with the curriculum and reinforce the truths conveyed on Sunday mornings.

Family Worship

Having regular family worship or a devotional time is important no matter the age of your children. This can be as simple as reading a passage of Scripture and praying together around the dinner table. Musically-gifted families can sing praise songs and hymns together. I also recommend young families use the extensive Family Time Materials resources available from FamiliesAlive. The Family Time Materials contain beautifully-illustrated Bible stories, fun family activities, and meaningful application ideas.

Leading Your Child to Christ

Jesus calls us to Himself in ways and at times specific to each individual. Because we are intentionally cooperating with the Holy Spirit in His enlivening work, we may be privileged to help our child "across the line of faith".

When my son, Stephen, was two years old, we were concluding his Bible storybook for the umpteenth time. The final story has to do with heaven. Stephen asked, "Mommy, how do I go to heaven?" It was there, on his bed, that I explained the good news to him. He prayed and asked Jesus to be "his forever friend." I was completely surprised by his ability to formulate the question and respond to the gospel at such an early age, and I'm in full-time ministry with children!

A few years later, I invited a children's evangelist to lead a special program at our church. He explained the gospel simply and winsomely to the children, extending them an invitation to receive Jesus as their Lord and Savior. As Stephen and I listened, I asked him what he thought of the message, and if that was a prayer he would like to pray. Somewhat indignant, he turned to me and said, "But Mommy, I already did that!" He not only responded to Christ as a two-year-old, but he clearly remembered this experience as a five-year-old. Certainly, God can call us to Himself at any age, and some children may not even remember those first steps of faith. Our responsibility as parents is simply to place them in the path of the Divine.

Prayer

Children need to learn that they can pray to God at any time, anywhere, about anything. When we pray and pay attention to the answers we receive from our prayers, our faith is strengthened.

We taught prayer to our children by reviewing the day's events with them at bedtime. We talked about the good and bad things that happened, and then thanked God for His graciousness to us in the positive aspects of the day, and to ask His wisdom to know how to deal with the negative circumstances we faced. This activity made prayer more personal and current to them. Keeping a prayer journal is an excellent way of recording our prayers and the answers we receive. All children need to see God as a "doer". They need to see that He is actively involved in the matters that most concern them and has the power to do something about it.

Keeping a photo book of people for whom we are praying is another way we can remember these individuals to God. Photos may be kept of family members, missionaries, friends, and significant others. An app such as *PrayerMate* or *Prayer Notes* is another great way to access prayers for mealtime, nighttime, mornings, car time, and more.

Another idea is to assign a day of the week to each family member as their special prayer day. The Shultz family has been doing this for years, and their children love having a specific day that they know they are being prayed for.

Blessing Your Children

The tradition of blessing your children beautifully conveys the love of God and the love of parents to their children. John Trent's book, *The Blessing*, provides a vast assortment of blessings to be spoken over children. As a child departs for school at the beginning of the day, or just before he drifts off to sleep at night, words of affirmation and God's promises assures the child that His heavenly Father is watching over him.

FamiliesAlive also provides an e-booklet, *How to Bless Your Children*, about this special tradition. It is a quick read and you can access it on their website (www.familiesalive.org) for free.

Stewardship

Jesus was concerned about the use of money and so should we be alerted to the tension between serving God and our earthly treasures. Parents can model the proper use of money by explaining to children what it means to give generously and cheerfully, to live responsibly within their means, and to save for future needs as they are able. Parents can teach children the joy of delayed gratification, and the satisfaction of earning and saving for a special object or experience. It is important for children to understand that their parents make decisions about money based on their relationship with Christ. Children need to know how their parents are giving sacrificially to Christian endeavors and why their parents make these decisions as a response of faith to the One who has graciously given us all things.

One tangible way to teach stewardship is to use the envelope system. When they receive their allowance, a cash gift, or babysitting money, they learn to split their money into the dedicated envelopes for tithing (10%), saving (40%), and spending (50%).

Service Projects

When I was in college, I was taught that fourth and fifth graders need to see God as a "doer" as part of their faith development. I now believe that we all need to see God as a "doer" in order for our faith to grow. Providing opportunities for our families to serve others as acts of spiritual service enlarges our hearts and provides us opportunities to cooperate with the Holy Spirit as He accomplishes His work in the world.

Our church provides opportunities for families to serve. Joining together with other families in larger projects builds community and teaches selflessness. In our own families, we can shop and deliver food to a local food pantry, stuff a shoebox full of gifts for Operation Christmas Child, sponsor a child through various Christian organizations, rake leaves or shovel snow for our neighbors. These are a few of the ways we can actively make a difference in our world and model the quality of service to our children. Serving together as a family is a particularly meaningful way to make our faith real in the home.

9

HECK OF A DEAL!

Several years ago, I was sent this email. I have no knowledge of its origin, but it's a gem for all parents to read. May it be an encouragement to you.

"I have seen, repeatedly, the breakdown of the cost of raising a child, but this is the first time I have seen the rewards listed this way. It's nice, really nice!!

According to FoxNews.com, the cost of raising a child from birth through age 17, based upon numbers from 2015, equals $233,610. Talk about sticker shock! That doesn't even touch college tuition.

But $233,610 isn't so bad if you break it down. It translates into $13,741.76 per year; $1,145.15 per month; $264.26 per week; and $37.75 per day.

Still, you might think the best financial advice says to not have children if you want to be "rich." It is just the opposite. What do you get for your $233,610?

Naming rights. First, middle, and last!

Glimpses of God every day.

Giggles under the covers every night.

More love than your heart can hold.

Butterfly kisses and Velcro hugs.

A hand to hold, usually covered with jam.

Endless wonder over rocks, ants, clouds, and warm cookies.

A partner for blowing bubbles, flying kites, building sand-castles, and skipping down the sidewalk in the pouring rain.

Someone to laugh yourself silly with no matter what the boss said or how your stocks performed that day.

For $233,610, you never have to grow up.

You get to finger-paint, carve pumpkins, play hide-and-seek, catch lightning bugs, and never stop believing in Santa Claus.

You have an excuse to keep reading your favorite children's stories, watching Saturday morning cartoons, going to Disney movies, and wishing on stars.

You get to frame rainbows, hearts, and flowers under refrigerator magnets and collect spray-painted noodle wreaths for Christmas, hand prints set in clay for Mother's Day, and cards with backward letters for Father's Day.

For $233,610, there is no greater bang for your buck.

You get to be a hero just for retrieving a Frisbee off the garage roof, taking the training wheels off the bike, removing a splinter, filling a wading pool, coaxing a wad of gum out of bangs, and coaching a baseball team that never wins but always gets treated to ice cream regardless.

You get a front row seat to history, witnessing the first step, first word, first bra, first date, and first time behind the wheel.

You get to be immortal.

You get another branch added to your family tree, and if you're blessed, a long list of limbs in your obituary called grandchildren.

You get an education in psychology, nursing, criminal justice, communications, and human sexuality that no college can match.

In the eyes of a child, you rank right up there with God.

You have all the power to heal a boo-boo, scare away the monsters under the bed, patch a broken heart, police a slumber party, ground them forever, and love them without limits, so one day they will, like you, love without counting the cost."

10

Final Encouragement

Effective parents model their faith to their children through word and deed. However, there is no formula for raising well-behaved, well-adjusted children. We are broken, fallen people raising broken, fallen children.

As your child reaches adulthood, he or she may reject every seed you have planted and pursue a different path in life, even if you did everything "right". I have witnessed heartbreaking circumstances unfold over and over in the lives of children of completely well-meaning, nurturing parents who have done their best to introduce their children to their Creator and Lord.

No matter what we do and no matter how sincere our efforts, we are not God. We cannot soften a person's heart and incline a person's will to their Heavenly Father. We cannot save our children. Only God, the Holy Spirit, can do that work of enlivening individuals. The reality of sin infecting all humans and our own free will lies at the core of this rejection.

Bringing our children to God in daily prayer is the best action we can take if we hope to see our children come to an awareness of true spiritual realities. He loves them even more than we; only He can powerfully and persuasively draw them to Himself in His timing. His will, His timing, and His plan are not subject to our approval or our timetable.

Above all, you can become an effective spiritual parent by focusing on your own relationship with your Heavenly Father. As you continually grow in your devotion to Him, He will transform your mind, soften your heart, and empower you through His Holy Spirit to serve as an example of the life-changing power of the gospel, not only for your own children but for the ever-changing world in which you live.

64225731R00061

Made in the USA
Middletown, DE
04 September 2019